IN THE SHADOW
OF THE TORNADO

IN THE SHADOW OF THE TORNADO

Stories and Adventures From the Heart of Storm Country

By Richard Bedard

GILCO PUBLISHING : NORMAN

Printed on acid-free paper in the United States of America.

First edition, 1996.
Second printing, 1997.

Gilco Publishing
P.O. Box 2175
Norman, Oklahoma 73070-2175

Copies may be ordered prepaid directly from the publisher. Please enclose $11.95 plus $3 for postage and handling. Oklahoma residents add $.90 for 7.5% sales tax.

ISBN 0-9649527-1-8
LCCN 95-81642

Cover photograph of the Cordell, Okla. "*Wizard of Oz*" tornado courtesy of the National Severe Storms Laboratory.
Cover design by Bill Cason and David, Randall & Yates, Graphic+Design

Blow wind, swell billow, and swim bark!
The storm is up, and all is on the hazard.

Shakespeare, *Julius Caesar*

Contents

Acknowledgments

There are many, many people to whom I owe a great deal of gratitude for helping to make this book happen. The fine people of Oklahoma are as warm and generous as any I have met in my many travels. In my attempts to schedule interviews in Woodward, I was refused only once. I dedicate this book to those brave tornado survivors, whose stories are full of extraordinary courage and resilience.

Readers of the rough manuscript gave me invaluable advice. Thanks to lay readers Bill Sherwood, Linda DiGiosaffatte, and Sean Beall. They helped smooth out the prose and steered me away from lapsing into "weatherman talk." I was truly fortunate to have had access to meteorologists of the caliber of Bob Davies-Jones, Keith Brewster, and Steve Hunter to make corrections and suggestions. Louise B. James graciously checked my history of Woodward (anyone with further interest in this town should peruse her very readable history, *Below Devil's Gap*).

While I acknowledge their contributions, any mistakes herein I take full responsibility for.

Further, I thank Rodger Harris and members of the Oklahoma Historical Society for accommodating me in my research—the historical society's newspaper collection on microfilm is a real treasure. Much of my material about Neil Ward and the history of the National Severe Storms Laboratory came courtesy of the History of Science Collections of the University of Oklahoma Libraries in Norman. And I must slip in here somewhere a thank you to my family for their support, and to Molly Griffis for good and timely counsel.

Last, there were people I interviewed and who assisted me that I am much indebted to, but some of whose names will appear only once in this book, in the list below. They were not forgotten; sometimes I was urged to trim names and stories to improve readability. The following is perhaps incomplete, but I have tried to include all, and apologize to anyone I overlooked: Calvin Anglin, Keith Ballard, Don Beckel, Douglas and Pauline Benbrook, Matt Biddle, Ruth Bohn, Donald Burgess, Marcella and Nyle Bynum, Charles Clark, Bob Conforth, Harold Conner, Mary Ann Cooper, Jim Cox, Ken Crawford, Betty Cullen, Elizabeth Cutler, Jerry Dalrymple, Eldon and Eileen Damron, Phil Davis, Virginia and Sam Davis, Gene and June Devine, Gertrude Devine, Ross Dixon, Chuck Doswell, Beryl and Joe Duer, Dale Durnell, Gary England, Vernon Enlow, Marty Feely, Pat Foster, Gloria Fothergill, Rick Fowler, Agnes Giddens (formerly Hutchison), George Goetzinger, Charles Goin Jr., Joe Golden, Lavera Haller, Bill Hauptman, Dave Hoadley, Noble Hunter, Thelma and Raymond Irwin, Edward Jessup, Fred Jordan, Kathy Kanak, Kevin Kelleher, Ed Kessler, Bert and Margaret Larason, Elsie Leonard, Jim Leonard, Martin Lisius, Mark Loftis, Donald Lynch, Harry Lynch, Tim Marshall, John D. and Bobbie Marston, Frankie McCreary, Mary Meacham, Alan Mitchell, Al Moller, Gene Moore, Mike Morgan, George and Winnie Mae Nelson, Paul Nelson, Claribel Niemeyer, Fred Norman, Betty Nosler (formerly Warriner), Panhandle-Plains Historical Museum, Marvella Parks, Garland Pendergraf, Beau and Sabrina Phillips, Jeff Piotrowski, Jim Purpura, Erik Rasmussen, Gene Rhoden, Father James Ross, Paul and Beverly Schoen, Gary Schneider, Thelma Schneider, Franklin Stecher, Jerry Straka, Ben Terry, Orlin Trego, Bob Ward, Jean Ward, Steve and Sue Weygandt, Dorothy Warriner, John D. Warriner, Doug Williams, Jim Williams, George Wood.

Introduction

Not so long ago, I couldn't have found the little town of Catoosa, Oklahoma, on a map, and I wouldn't have known where to start looking. Then on April 24, 1993, I was in a downtown Oklahoma City library and stepped out into a warm, windy day. In the distance I saw it, a heaped cloud shining white, streaking to the northeast. It moved so fast that—this is the best way to describe it—it's like someone was yanking that thing along on a wire.

Right then it didn't look menacing, and I didn't know that parts of Oklahoma were under a tornado watch.

The next morning the *Sunday Oklahoman* headline came as a complete shock: "TULSA TWISTER DEATH TOLL 10" (this figure proved mistaken; actually seven died). A week earlier I'd had a strange nightmare, the first of many during the two years I spent researching and writing this book. I was standing among others in a street, all of us staring fixedly at a tornado on the horizon. A moment passed, and it turned out to be a dark shaft of rain. We felt a palpable sense of relief. Then, there it was, a huge black tornado barreling straight into downtown, no time left to run . . .

I scanned the newspaper article and decided to go to Tulsa. A few hours later, my little Toyota sedan was crawling in a long stream of sightseers up Highway 66 into the river-port town of Catoosa, a Tulsa suburb especially hard hit. Sunshine winked off sheet metal that draped denuded tree limbs like toilet paper after a frat prank. A concrete mobile home pad was whisked clean, as if a whimsical owner had decided to leave suddenly during the night. And you could only pray that those drivers of cars brutally flipped onto their roofs had gotten out in time.

I walked around, looked, and listened.

"It was so black," a man said, grasping for words, "I don't know how you can describe black. And the clouds looked like God had a humongous churn." There was the woman whose 240-pound husband lay on top of her like a human paperweight as the winds pulled off the country club roof, the oblong hail the size of a human fist, the storm towers twisted "like garbage bag ties."

A man gardening heard a cannonade of thunder, 15 straight minutes. Sprinkling rain drove him inside. He showered, then went to the window to check his slender Golden Delicious apple tree, his "weather gauge to the world." When white, the tree indicated snow. When it leaned over, the wind was blowing. He looked out. The tree was gone. A minute later, he was flying through his house clutching a chest of drawers. He luckily survived, unhurt.

From that day in Catoosa, I also remember a quiet image, of a heifer standing with the sun setting at its back in a ruddy glow. The animal was fearfully still, as if somewhere deep inside its mammalian brain an alarm was going off, a reminder of a hell that had visited at exactly 24 hours before. The animal seemed to be bracing itself, waiting for a roaring wind to return.

It was a meaningful image because, after a bad twister hits the state, there's a heightened awareness and fear. Oklahomans confront anew the reality of where they live. It struck me that living in storm country meant more than becoming a victim one day. It was also the threat of becoming one, and harboring that thought on a spring day when storms raked the state in long lines, like celestial wrecking crews.

And, in a strange turn, I found that this springtime threat actually attracted people to Oklahoma. They love the tempests, and all the grumbling and flashing and violently shearing currents of wind. They call themselves storm chasers, and they too were part of the Catoosa experience. Some of them tailing the thunderhead almost blundered underneath the forming tornado.

In writing this book, I decided to structure it around these three groups, if you will. In Part One, the victims tell the story of the Woodward tornado, the deadliest in state history. Part Two shifts the focus to the general threat of the tornado and to how ordinary Oklahomans have come to be protected by the umbrella of what may be the best, most aggressive severe weather warning system in the world. Finally Part Three turns to the storm chasers, starting with research meteorologists who boldly ventured out seeking answers to a maddening atmospheric puzzle.

There are plenty of what I think are incredible stories and adventures here, but in trying for a balance between sensitivity and an often unpleasant reality, I've trimmed a few details. The science I hope is fairly simple and digestible. Anyone wanting a more complete treatment of storm behavior and structure is welcome to consult the bibliography.

Oh, one more thing about Catoosa: from one hard luck neighborhood I picked up a souvenir, a twisted stop sign post. Its rigid metal curls with almost the easy smoothness of a strip of formed pasta. I can't begin to conceive of designing a machine capable of doing this. But the wind wrought this curiosity, that same wind that trips through a meadow and gently sways the stems of bright wild flowers, or sends wee ripples shivering across a pond.

What is wind, where does it come from, where does it go?

The nineteenth-century poet Christina Rossetti wrote in sprightly verse:

Who has seen the wind?
Neither you nor I:
But when the trees bow down their heads,
The wind is passing by.

And sometimes, in the middle of Tornado Alley, those trees hold onto their heads for dear life.

Woodward, 1947

1

First Strike

It all began unremarkably enough, on a spring day in 1947. A cold, dry air mass was born, probably over the ice-caked reaches of Siberia. The air mass was huge, but blocked from moving by a high-pressure "dam" of air. Before long, the dam crumbled. The liberated blob of chilly air set sail on prevailing winds over the Pacific Ocean toward the western coast of the United States. Little did anyone know, hell would soon arrive with the Siberian Express.

Sprawling over hundreds of thousands of square miles, it crossed into California. On its leading edge swirled a weak low-pressure system. In this low—which covered an area larger than Arizona—wind and clouds spiraled in a counterclockwise flow toward the center, like water circling an emptying bathtub drain. The cold air mass and low-pressure region didn't linger very long. A high-altitude jet stream hurried them eastward.

Their passage did not go unnoticed. A 30-mile-an-hour breeze whistled through telephone lines in one southern California town that had been almost calm just 24 hours earlier. Near the center of the low, thunderstorms sprouted in southwestern Utah. Government meteorologists who consulted their finely detailed, coded weather maps could see that the system was swiftly marching across the country. Moreover, highs usher in clear blue skies, but lows stir up storms. They knew they had a troublemaker on their hands.

Unsettled weather certainly looked likely in the Texas Panhandle. The Siberian Express shoving in from the west was

about to collide with a body of warm, moist air coursing up from
the Gulf of Mexico. If the cold air mass proved to be a match,
here was the dynamite. Yet the official forecast for April 9, 1947,
for northwestern Oklahoma (which borders on the Texas Panhandle) hardly suggested a dangerous situation shaping up. In
retrospect its blandness seems eerie: "Showers and thunderstorms with moderate to heavy amounts of rain this afternoon,
tonight and Thursday . . . mild temperatures, low tonight 48–55."

Just after midnight on April 9, the Panhandle city of Amarillo reported overcast skies and a temperature of 50 degrees. As
the day wore on, the two bodies of greatly contrasting air—one
cold and dry, the other warm and moist—converged from their
different directions. In what seemed to the untrained eye like a
promising development, the sun broke through the cloud-filled
Amarillo sky. The heat warmed spiny yuccas and twisted juni-
pers, but also destabilized the blanket of moist air bottled up
near the ground. By late afternoon, it was simmering danger-
ously. The pressure-cooker instability wouldn't last long. The
atmosphere was getting ready to pop.

It did, in piles of cloud that lunged vertically before being
tilted and knocked flat by high upper winds. Each failure served
a purpose. Clouds grow better in wet environments, so succeed-
ing towers were able to make better headway. At last the med-
dling wind lost in dramatic fashion. Thick, creamy-white columns jetted up. They bubbled and foamed, burgeoning like some
kind of runaway nuclear fission.

A giant cloud formed. It reached great heights, up into the
distant stratosphere. Off its crown spread downstream an anvil,
a flat deck of ice crystals flung out by intense winds. The storm,
a good ten miles deep, threw the plains into sudden darkness
like a moving eclipse. And the movement was unmistakable, a
brisk 40 miles an hour to the northeast.

From a distance this simple confection of water and air
looked as solid as an island sculpted from marble. Closer in the
illusion dissolved. The cloud was evolving and mutating with
dizzying speed. It was actually a rapidly changing weather factory. Lightning flashed, then thunder rolled through gypsum
canyons below. Raindrops formed and fell in waves.

The central trunk underwent the most startling transfor-

mation. Once sprawling and disorganized, it became smooth and
tight, like something run through a cosmic lathe. The wide updraft of air feeding this floating giant wasn't only streaking
upwards. It was turning in steady revolutions. The storm was
twisting around itself.

Near Amarillo appeared another surprise. An odd-looking
protuberance lowered below the low, dark base. It was a rotating
collar of cloud that resembled a wheel or flaring suction mouth.
A curious sort of activity then commenced. Just below the wheel,
cloud tags seemed to snatch at each other, clumping together. At
first this looked like harmless atmospheric prankishness, then
something sinister took form. A funnel was sliding out of the sky.

Dirt spiked up when it touched the ground. It raced off beside railroad tracks that ran northeast, and headed on a beeline
toward White Deer. The tornado did not travel very long alone,
unobserved. It slipped behind a 61-car Santa Fe Railway freight
train that was leisurely chugging into White Deer to pick up
more empty cars. At a quarter of six, their paths crossed un-
forgettably.

When the caboose darkened, the curious conductor went
toward the rear platform to look out. The floor beneath his feet
shifted. The tornado had seized his train. It jerked up the steel
cars and jackknifed them together like flimsy toys. Brake lines
snapped and bunks, stoves, chairs, and clothes rained down on
crewmen. It threw down wreckage for half a mile beside the
tracks, then bore down on a farmhouse and pulled it off the
ground. A dazed locomotive fireman watching this later told a
newspaper reporter, "The house lifted a few feet in the air, then
hung there and shook like a fish being lifted out of water." Then
the building appeared to explode.

High atop an eight-story grain elevator under construction, a
few dozen laborers were dumbfounded by this unfolding spectacle. They recovered their senses enough to realize they were
about to become the next victims. Some managed to scramble
down a ladder. Those who didn't cowered on the hardening concrete, waiting to be plucked off and hurled to their deaths. The
men were spared when the shrieking twister weaved 100 yards
to the north, tearing down the scaffolding around the elevator as
it went.

It raged northeast, appearing ghostly white after its passage because the sun lit it from the west. Moving away and weakening, it inspired less fear. The tornado thinned and seemed to drag, to dislocate from its parent cloud. It became a tenuous, whipping umbilical cord linking sky and soil, hardly capable of toppling even an old barn. Dying, the rope grew yet skinnier until it dissipated, its malevolent energy spent.

White Deer had escaped with little damage and few injuries. A new path, 70 yards wide, cut across town. It was rudely marked by wrecked barns, garages, chicken houses, outbuildings, and a few homes, all amid a melting litter of golf-ball-sized hailstones. A woman who had been in the farmhouse nursed fresh scratches and bruises, as did a few train crewmen. At least the storm had passed, they all consoled themselves, and had lost its most vicious feature, the tornado.

But the real horror was just beginning. Instead of fading quietly, the storm feasted on the rich layer of warm, moist air in the environment it moved through—and gathered strength. For the moment, nothing spun on the ground, but miles above the earth, the muscular core was still making its revolutions. A severe thunderstorm can lay down a succession of tornadoes. Over the short grasses and treeless solitude of the High Plains, a new, wider wheel-shaped cloud pushed down.

It produced an incredible sight. Five spinning columns snaked down and moved across the barren land. A pair of railroad signalmen gaped at the twister gang, pirouetting in a circle and nearing fast. The workers dove into a culvert just before a mighty wind swept over the tracks, knocking a motor car off the rails and sucking up the signal station.

The pack of whirls swirled on over open country. The occasional eyewitness could only look on in speechless amazement. One man wasn't sure what to think of the beautiful, reddish-gold cloud, sprouting writhing coils, that passed before the sun. On touching down, each appeared to snap off from the glowing cloud, then played itself out. They looked like cave stalactites, he thought.

What he didn't know was that he had spied a tornado so large and so strong it had evolved into the deadly multiple-vortex state. Seen from afar, the spinning vortices appeared tranquil and hypnotic. Up close, they were killers. Their winds topped 200 miles an hour. What devastation they could wreak was known only after the tornado skirted the towns of Pampa, Miami, and Canadian. The luck of the Panhandle was about to run out in a small settlement near the Oklahoma border.

Glazier it was called, a once thriving local trading hub that had always persevered in the face of adversity and changing times. Even after its economic importance as a rail station waned, even after three blazes in different decades destroyed major businesses and the central railroad depot, Glazier stubbornly hung on. After all, the fires never took anything. Then the winds did.

Later, survivors remembered light rain falling, then hail, and feeling vaguely unsettled. A mounting roar was heard to the southwest. It could have been the evening freight train, but the noise reached an earsplitting crescendo, as though the train was about to come crashing over the porch. To a no doubt God-fearing man this unearthly sound suggested the "mad screaming of ten thousand devils."

Glazier never had a chance. Board by board it flew apart. It was scrubbed off the face of the land. Washing machines tumbled out of the sky like footballs, half a mile from their laundry. Railway signals vanished without a trace. Windmill towers snapped in half. Everything was crashing and flying, from houses to barbed wire to bark stripped from fence posts.

As the town reeled in shock, the tornado—now a staggering one and a half miles wide—slammed into the Texas border town of Higgins. There was no longer anything playful or gentle about this storm. It was fully mature, with an unchecked wrath. Windows crashed in all around a terrified woman recuperating at the Higgins hospital. A loud, clacking rumble left behind a business district burning in the dusk. Fireballs leaped high. Contemplating this apocalyptic scene, she understandably assumed that the world must be coming to an end.

She was not alone in finding images too unreal to be believed. A four-ton lathe lay in two pieces, ripped like tin foil. Naked men, women, and children, divested of their clothing by ravenous winds, stumbled blindly through streets clogged with rubble. A house straddled a highway. A bizarre tale (perhaps untrue, for fact and fiction were no longer easily distinguishable) later circulated of an elderly woman found dead, a 16-penny nail sunk into the center of her forehead, her eyeballs plucked out. A swath of utter ruin in its wake, the storm slipped into northwestern Oklahoma. Dusk changed to deep night. At 7:28 P.M., a weather observer at the Gage airport scribbled in his log, using abbreviations, "barometer unsteady, thunderstorm overhead, vivid lightning, cloud-to-cloud, cloud-to-ground." Hail peppered the airfield. To the east, the tornado moved by, unobserved.

In a gabled two-and-a-half-story white house east of Gage, Margaret Larason had, until then, passed an uneventful evening. She was pretty, with soft, slanted gray eyes, and seven months pregnant with her third child. Her doctor had delivered guarded news that afternoon. Her birth canal was obstructed. She would need a Caesarean section. He warned her not to do anything to risk inducing premature labor.

That day, her outdoor activity consisted mainly of planting baby cedars and a pair of large lilac bushes on their tidy house lot. Those tasks weren't too strenuous. Hired hand Arlo Pittman, who lived with his wife and their baby son in a small stuccoed house just a short way down the road, did the backbreaking farm chores. The Larasons had milking cows, cattle, chickens, hogs, and a thousand-acre field of wheat to tend to.

The storm was far away when Margaret fixed supper for Tim, six, and Anne, five. In a few days Bert, who served with the Oklahoma Legislature, was returning for the weekend. As usual, she expected her husband to try to cram a week's worth of farm work into a few days. She took solace in the fact the Legislature met for less than half a year. And lawmakers could legally draw pay for only 60 days, a good incentive for them to finish up and go home.

After supper, hail clicked on the roof. Margaret tried to call Bert to share her new concern about her pregnancy, but the phone was dead. She took the children out onto the covered porch that ringed the house. They watched milky hailstones bounce and skip across a concrete sidewalk. With no forewarning, their cocker spaniel nervously bolted past her, through the front door. How peculiar, she thought. He wasn't a house dog.

The animal darted under a bed in the northeast bedroom and refused to budge.

Puzzled, she went about her nightly routine, putting Tim and Anne to bed. Under his pillow Tim stashed a prized flashlight, a gift from an aunt. Her children tucked in at last, Margaret went downstairs. She was annoyed, but not all that surprised when the lights went out. She lit a kerosene lamp, then Tim and Anne padded in barefoot.

"My window blew out and made a terrible noise," Anne said.

Alone, Margaret climbed the staircase, using a flashlight to guide her step. She intended to cover the broken window, but what she discovered on the second floor amazed her. It was like stepping into another world. Wind tunneled loudly through the hallway, and in Anne's bedroom, rain poured through the shattered window. She played the flashlight beam over white organdy curtains, flapping nearly horizontal. A cradle holding a doll scraped across the floor. Margaret stood in stunned silence, then the door slammed behind her.

She knew then she had to hurry. She struggled with the bedroom door, but the wind firmly pressed against it. Panic gripped her, a sickening feeling of helplessness, a fear of being separated from her children. Mustering all her strength, she managed to muscle the door open. She fled down the stairs and grabbed an armful of blankets from a closet.

"Get under the kitchen table," she ordered the children in a trembling voice. Wide-eyed, Tim and Anne obeyed. She covered them with blankets. Too far pregnant to fit underneath herself, she sat in a chair under a blanket. Only the storm could be heard, raging and shaking their house, filling their ears with its wild fury. They were in the belly of the beast. An especially loud noise startled her, then stillness prevailed.

Finally, she thought with nervous relief, but no sooner was she about to relax than the winds surged again with incredible violence. The gable roof creaked and strained, and the howling scream outside rose to a wicked pitch. There was nothing she could yell to comfort her children, not over that. Somehow the house resisted this second onslaught, and calm returned. She breathed more easily. Shaken but unhurt, the Larasons threw aside the blankets.

There was no time to exult in their good fortune; Margaret smelled butane leaking from one of the copper fuel lines for the stove. There must be more damage, she thought, and resolved to drive to Fargo to call Bert. She halted at the front door. That loud noise had been their porch. It was ripped up and pinned flat like skirting against the house. Without that shield, she realized, flying debris could have blown in and killed them.

She waited for Arlo Pittman to rescue them, assuming he would come check on her. When she glimpsed his car headlights moving tentatively down the road, she wondered why he hadn't come sooner. After Pittman freed her and the children by opening a side door blocked by bookshelves, she found out why. The storm was worse than she had imagined. The hired hand related how he scooped his baby boy out of bed as the roof flew away and chunks of plaster tumbled down. To reach her, he had to drive through torrents of rain and steer around fallen utility poles snapped like toothpicks.

With a flashlight, they went outside and hunted for the butane control valve, stepping gingerly through knee-deep shingles and debris. Outbuildings were destroyed and a full 1500-gallon water storage tank was gone. A small metal windmill anchored in cement was bent like a horseshoe, its revolving wheel stuffed under the front bumper of the car. They located the butane valve and quickly turned it off, before a random spark could trigger a catastrophic explosion.

Preliminary reports of the tornado strikes on the High Plains reached Oklahoma City, where Bert Larason heard of the news after a dinner with some colleagues and an oil lobbyist. Initial accounts mentioned only Higgins and Glazier. He never entertained seriously the notion that his farm was damaged. Tornadoes don't travel that far, he reasoned. Then, to his shock, the phone call came.

Early the next morning, he and a nephew set out from Oklahoma City. At noon, they drove up to the farm. Margaret greeted him, but they spoke little. Looking around, dispirited, he was ready to accept this as an omen. Maybe it was time to pack it in and move on. Maybe it was time to leave a land that had, at best, proved marginally fertile and that constantly tested a man's mettle and ingenuity.

His farm was a shambles. Befuddled hens and roosters perched at dusk on the jumble of boards that had been their coop. Wandering shoats and hogs had to be herded onto a flatbed wheat truck, pressed into service as a temporary holding pen. The twister had even lifted the house roof and lowered it with the rafters lined up on the wrong side of the joists and hay jammed under the eaves.

In the end, the Larasons did stay, but never forgot the storm—not that such a thing was possible. That summer, miles of scattered tin debris glinted in wheat fields. It flattened combine tires, so a field hand was assigned to ride in a trailer behind a combine and jump out to pick up any trash he spotted. Anne's doll and cradle surfaced in a pasture, a chilling reminder of how narrowly the Larason children escaped. And on June 14, 1947, Linda Larason was born. Her doctor attributed the baby's cross, nervous disposition to disturbance in the womb.

From White Deer into Oklahoma, the tornado left a trail of splintered homes and ruined lives. Towns glowed with fires, and smoke hung overhead like a noxious fog. Ambulance sirens wailed as families quietly tried to fathom what had gone so terribly wrong, so quickly. They tried to remember the last words from an uncle or daughter who would never speak again.

Hard as it was to believe, the tornado had not done its worst. By 8:30 P.M., two and a half hours after the storm first exhibited its capacity for violence over the Texas Panhandle, it was still moving steadily and powerfully to the northeast. There weren't any large towns in northwestern Oklahoma, except Woodward. And that's exactly where the tornado was heading.

2

Woodward Braces

In 1947, 5,500 people proudly called the town of Woodward home. This prairie community was nestled among low sand hills and wide wheat fields. Along its northern border flowed the North Canadian River, which ran slow and shallow in August and fast and swollen in spring. The town got its name, so went one story, after a buffalo hunter slogged through quicksand in crossing the river. For those who followed he posted a sign with the cryptic message that it was miles to civilization, but three feet to hell. His signature: "R.M. Woodward."

One of the most thrilling events in Woodward's history came a few years after that hunter's mishap, in 1893, during the largest land run ever in what was to become Oklahoma. Men on horseback swarmed over an immense strip of land, gaily firing pistols into the air. They galloped into town and claimed 160-acre plots. Those hiding overnight in canyons and caverns who only pretended to charge in with the others got the nickname "Sooners."

The great land giveaway completed the displacement in the area of long-suffering Indian tribes who had been attacked by United States troops and coerced into treaties. They were most effectively subdued through the slaughter of the buffalo, an important source of food, clothing, and shelter. White hunters killed untold thousands of the beasts, stripping their hides—or sometimes taking only the tongues, a delicacy—and leaving the large carcasses to spoil in the sun.

To replace the buffalo, settlers introduced longhorn and cattle to graze the rich wild grasses, and Woodward figured prominently into the new economy. Rollicking cowboys drove their livestock to its railroad yards, which became a major shipping point for cattle. The bustling young cow town soon had a post office, barber shop, feed store, general store, and two-story hotel, as well as a red-light district and twice as many saloons as churches.

No one would deny Woodward had a tough side. Men gambled on cockfights in bullet-pocked bars, spit tobacco on dusty sidewalks, and tossed back a drink or two (or three or four). One of its early citizens was the flamboyant attorney Temple Houston, son of Texas Revolution hero Sam Houston. The younger Houston roamed the dirt-packed streets with authority. Tall and handsome, with a taste for hard liquor, he ate fist-sized chili peppers like apples and shot a drunken farmer who allegedly spit in his son's face.

Some of the town's toughness was related not to gun-slinging, but to the harsh, inhospitable environment. Splashes of wild flowers like Indian paintbrush and wild verbena brightened the broad surrounding fields, but just as familiar were clumps of scraggly gray-green sagebrush. A few hardy pines, cedars, elms, and golden cottonwoods endured a climate of too much wind and too little water.

The land was not lush and fertile, but Woodward stubbornly grew. It survived the Great Depression, when self-made princes turned into paupers overnight. A local bank president living in a lovely colonial-style brick mansion with white porch pillars lost everything in 1932. Before the decade ended, he was seen at a hotel, virtually penniless, smoking cigar butts with the aid of a toothpick.

And it survived the Dust Bowl days. For years, old-timers told of how the worst cloud swept in on a day remembered as Black Sunday: April 14, 1935. A roiling black wall of dirt sent fleeing before it birds, insects, and other creatures. As it passed, the sun dimmed to a faraway glow. Chickens roosted at noon. No matter how tightly windows and doors were sealed with wet towels and blankets, fine dirt filtered in and had to be scooped up each morning. In summer the town was barren and parched, with one wall of the nickel-and-ten-cent store devoted to a dust mask display.

In a poem about life during the miserable Dust Bowl era, a member of a pioneer family by the name of Esther Laubach wrote:

The clouds sweep down like vampires
They smother and choke every breath
And you curse and strike out blindly
At such a torturous living death.

Despite the hardships of the 1930s, people were able to distract themselves with everyday pleasures. There were still beauty contests and band concerts, and ice cream socials in the park. A sackful of six juicy hamburgers sold for 25 cents at the town's first drive-in restaurant. In the open air behind the library, preachers blasted sin and sang the praises of virtue. And this rough-and-tumble prairie town never abandoned faith in a dream of progress.

After World War II, and the return of its victorious young men from what all agreed was a necessary and just war, Woodward could turn inward again to nourish that dream. A bright future beckoned. By 1947 it had an airport, a paved main street, and the Elks Rodeo, billed as the "toughest of them all." On the edge of town, the United States Field Station studied farming practices and ways to improve crops.

That spring, townspeople parted the pages of the newspaper to learn that Jackie Robinson had broken the color barrier in professional baseball. Henry Ford, father of the mass-produced automobile, died in his Dearborn, Michigan, home of a cerebral hemorrhage. In a news brief, a starry-eyed professor waxed optimistic about the newly liberated power of the atom. Within five years, he predicted, an atomic pellet the size of a pencil eraser tossed into a furnace would heat a house for decades.

But the real story in Woodward was a possible nationwide telephone worker strike. Unhappy with their salaries, union members were threatening a walkout. If they did, people in Woodward wouldn't cope happily. Phone service had tied together the community ever since a local company installed the first network. In fact, one of the first customers fumed after an operator failed to call in an hour, as had been promised, when it was time to remove baking bread from her oven.

The advent of the telephone also gave rise to a primitive

warning system. Operators in neighboring towns alerted one
another to approaching severe weather. Every so often a winter
storm coughed up enough snow to paralyze the county and even
bury a locomotive, but more common were damaging spring
thunderstorms that laid down tornadoes, or "cyclones," as they
were then called. According to Indian legend, Woodward was
protected from tornadoes because it lay in a valley of sorts, a
wide, flat bowl bracketed by gently rising hills.

The awful proof of how wrong they were came on a dreary
day that dawned cool, windy, and drizzly. Such weather was
nothing out of the ordinary. April was a fickle month, sometimes
wet and blustery, sometimes summery warm. That morning a
mailman laid empty mail sacks over two open boxes of sleepy-
eyed baby chicks in the back of his pickup truck. He drove
through town to make the delivery, past tall American elms
leafing out next to brick-and-tile buildings.

The nation's first telephone strike was by then in its third
day. When talks broke down, three hundred thousand workers
left their posts to picket. Instead of "Number, please," Woodward
merchants and housewives picked up their telephones to hear,
"Accepting emergency calls only, due to labor difficulties." A
skeleton crew of supervisors staffed the Ninth Street office, while
strikers marched back and forth in the mist outside, waving
protest signs. They didn't stay out any longer than they had to,
because a strong wind from the southeast made the dampness
very unpleasant.

There was something strange in the air, too. No one could
breathe very well, what with the wind whipping dirt about and a
general oppressiveness. People were angry and nervous at work.
Fishermen who flicked their lines into the river discovered that
the fish weren't biting. A cat tried to nudge her kittens inside,
birds flew northeast, cattle huddled close to their shed, chickens
roosted early. Farmers, who knew well to heed strange animal
behavior, braced themselves for a storm.

Early in the evening, an overcast sky replaced the mist. A
murky sun peeked out between the horizon and the cloud layer.
Small, shredded clouds, like low-flying wraiths, hurried north.
Before yielding to the moon, the sun made a beautiful, eerie
splash in crimson and deep copper. Then came a new, dazzling

attraction to the southwest. Lightning forked through an approaching high-banked thunderstorm that promised to be a gusher, or in prairie vernacular, a real "toad strangler."

South of Woodward, veterinarian David Jacobson was watching it. He wasn't a native of the region, but had learned to respect the occasionally explosive weather. Jacobson, born to immigrant parents, grew up on Coney Island in New York. He worked briefly on the New York Stock Exchange floor as a messenger, then after the market crashed in 1929, he went to Kansas to study veterinary medicine. He got a degree, married, and eventually moved to take a job in Woodward. He liked the town, even when roused from bed at 3 A.M. to tend to a sick animal. To the meek rancher standing uncomfortably at the door, worried about having woken the doctor, Jacobson would say, "I had to answer the doorbell, anyway."

On April 9, he was treating a sick cow when he saw the magnificent long black cloud. Sunlight shone on either side of the solid, advancing wall that was snapping up dust, as if someone was vigorously sweeping a dirty floor. He drove home with it following him.

He wasn't the only one from Woodward watching with some apprehension. Lightning, not that distant anymore, strobed with such frequency that it made the eye ache. The bright, ever-changing lattice flickered like throbbing veins. Those who viewed the angry brow of the glowering thunderhead, hardly able to release its mounting charges fast enough, could not but worry about what lay at its dark heart.

3

"Get Down . . . Tornado!"

From his bed, John Warriner stared through the window in awe. Ball lightning was scooting down the power lines from the Oklahoma Gas and Electric station and disappearing north. The bright orbs materialized every few seconds and zipped off into the night. A loud, tremulous boom of thunder instantly followed. John, 13, marveled at the display.

Tonight the entertainment was clearly outside, not in. The big brown Zenith radio (one of his chores was to charge the car battery that powered it at the corner service station) had crackled and popped with static. His father had been disappointed. Arthur Warriner Sr., a ruddy-faced former railroad carpenter, had several abiding pleasures. One was baseball, which always baffled his wife Dorothy, who never understood why a grown man would work hard all day, then disappear for a few hours in the evening to streak around base paths and squat in the dirt as a team catcher. Even after their wedding ceremony, Arthur rushed off to play baseball—peculiar behavior, she thought at the time with more than a bit of dismay. Another of his great loves was settling back into a comfortable chair at night and listening to the radio weave its magic. He especially liked the ghoulish 30-minute weekly program *Inner Sanctum Mysteries*.

The Warriners lived on Tenth Street on the north side of Woodward in a modest one-story house onto which Arthur had just added a living room. It was a project undertaken out of the strictest sort of practical necessity. They badly needed more bedroom space, what with the arrival of their sixth child in the

fall of 1945. Probably the family was poor by the material stan-
dards of the well-to-do, but they knew that they were rich in
some important, intangible sense of the word. Without a great
deal of effort, they managed to be happy together. Small hands
gleefully snatched at Dorothy's loaves of bread, steaming hot out
of the oven. Birthday parties meant the simple delight of pulling
homemade taffy. Almost every night flocks of neighborhood kids
gathered to soar on the swings hanging from the mulberry trees,
or roll barrel hoops or play kick the can on the dead-end street.

John was the third oldest of the children. He was a good-
looking, vigorous boy with dark eyes and a fondness for playing
pranks. He liked being outdoors, whether fishing, hunting, or
looking for Indian arrowheads. Sometimes, after a cleansing
rain, he strolled through plowed fields. He bent his head and
scanned the soil. Spying an arrowhead, he would triumphantly
snatch up the hard, flat rock, then go back to his search.

On this April night he was thankful to be inside, safely
watching the balls of lightning skate down power lines to twinkle
out of sight. He could see several miles up the North Canadian
River. At that distance, receding pinpricks of incandescence were
still visible. Then, after blackness swallowed each in turn, another blinding flash tore loose from the sky above the power
plant.

In downtown Woodward, a different weather phenomenon
preoccupied a drugstore owner. He was chatting with a local
restaurant proprietor about tornado damage in Oklahoma and
Missouri. In a front-page newspaper photo, the walls of a house
were missing, but the beds behind them unscathed. A soda jerk,
who was finished wiping down booths and stainless steel trim in
preparation for the after-movie rush, professed amazement that
a wind of that force didn't tear up the beds. Oh, the men said,
stranger sights have been witnessed: wheat straws stuck like
darts in trees, chickens plucked clean of feathers. Such winds
obey their own inscrutable laws. They might rip up a well-built
house but not disturb a full tray of delicate wine glasses on a
tablecloth. As voices rose in the drugstore, a stiff wind gusted
down Main Street.

Not far away, at the Oasis steakhouse, a waitress was trou-
bled. She failed to notice as orders backed up. Agnes Hutchison

was 28, a mother of two, with a sturdy build and a mane of thick hair that tumbled onto her shoulders. She was bright and sensible, and knew well enough to heed her intuition, which was nagging her. Before sunset, she had glimpsed the cloud, still a good ways off, rising like a mountain over the sheet-flat expanse of the Texas Panhandle. Agnes tried to call home, but the operator refused to patch through a nonemergency call. Cursing the telephone strike, she returned to her tables. Her anxiety deepened when Olan never showed up. He always dropped by with Jimmie Lee and Roland. He sipped coffee and they talked of the day's events, then he left to put the boys to bed.

Where was he? Her thoughts kept straying to her family, and their home that Olan had built with his own hands. It was only 12 by 16 feet at first. In those simple days, an orange crate served as a cabinet, a two-burner coal-oil stove sufficed for cooking, and from scraps of wood Olan fashioned everything from picture frames and book ends to shelves. She didn't have a job then and used to pull Roland in his kiddie wagon to a pasture and dawdle away hours picking wild flowers.

Agnes went outdoors and paced nervously up and down a step. She studied the sky. The thunderhead loomed blacker and larger. Something wasn't right. Restless and worried, she reentered the Oasis. Her boss greeted her by snapping that she ought to look after her orders. She did, hurrying onto the main floor. A smile masked her uneasy thoughts. She didn't want to be there and her house was only a few blocks away. If only she could break free of her six-to-midnight shift . . .

Even small children sensed something was amiss. A contest of wills was being played out between one mother and her four-year-old son. Thelma Irwin wanted Joe T. to go to bed, but he wouldn't. She wasn't sure how to handle his disobedience. They were the only two family members still awake. Her husband Raymond, a lean, mild-mannered truck line agent who worked odd shifts unloading and checking freight deliveries, was dozing on the enclosed sleeping porch. Jennifer slumbered in her crib. And Joe Thomas, like an affectionate puppy, trailed behind her.

It would have been adorable, except she knew he was scared. So was she. Earlier, the wind had blown so hard that when she mailed back a pair of overalls (a gift for Joe T., but a size too small) to a friend in Kansas, she told the kids to stay in the car. When visible, the sun was ugly, all hazy and dirty. Later she put out empty milk bottles on the front porch for the delivery man. A thought struck her with indisputable clarity: "If I leave them out, they're just going to get broken." Yet she did.

At last she scolded Joe T. and ordered him to bed. He trudged reluctantly through the open French doors from the dining room into the bedroom he shared with baby Jennifer. Tree crowns frothed beyond the sash window. On the canvas window shade Thelma had painted a merry legion of Mother Goose characters, including an innocent, cherubic Little Boy Blue curled up and sleeping by a haystack. She often read stories to the children and pointed to the figures in illustration, but this night brimmed with a menace that a gentler world could not dispel. To calm Joe T., she had him say his prayers. When she looked in again, he was doing just that.

"Jesus, I'm scared," he said, praying fervently. "Jesus, take care of me. Take care of momma."

He was not the only one to appeal to the mercy of a higher power. At one of 16 town churches holding Wednesday night services, a minister acknowledged the fear in the faces before him. Yes, something was wrong, he said, then asked the congregation to step forward and pray. A few silent prayers were probably uttered as well among the hundreds of filmgoers in downtown theaters. They were rapidly losing interest in the endings to *The Devil on Wheels* at the Terry and *Rage in Heaven* at the Woodward.

In the Woodward movie house, Orlin Trego's right ear was popping and bubbling. It had been sensitive to air pressure changes ever since some fisticuffs in Virginia while he was in Officer Candidate School. When he intervened one weekend to defend two girls being harassed by four soldiers, they turned on him, furious. Trego, a big man, slugged three of them, then they knocked him down. They kicked him, fracturing his skull and perforating his right eardrum. The men were deserters, so Trego emerged from the scuffle with a letter of commendation—and an ear to rival a home barometer.

He whispered to his wife to expect a storm. After a quick look outside at all the intense lightning in the distance, he reported it was going to be a big one. Trego wondered if they should leave, but she reasoned that the theater was better constructed than their house. An air conditioner on top of the building began banging about, then the images on the screen blinked off. Everyone waited uncomfortably in the dark. Across town, the owner of both movie theaters had to jump in his car and drive over. On his short ride, the theater owner noticed with alarm the overhead cloud, low and thick and black as ink. It looked as if he could reach up and cut it with a knife. At the theater he threw the power breaker to restore the electricity, then drove back to a church where he was screening a 16-millimeter home movie from Easter. One child in that film would not survive the night.

From a town 25 miles southeast of Woodward, a telephone operator called her counterpart.

"There is a black cloud over Woodward," she said. "It looks terrible."

"I haven't had time to look," came the reply.

No longer did anyone have to look. Changes could be heard and felt, like the strong wind blowing from the south that suddenly shifted to the east, then to the southwest. Rain fell hard, hail drummed down. Each stopped, to make way for an unnatural calm that descended swiftly, like a moment of dead silence before an explosion.

A man driving north of Woodward was perturbed when his engine started missing and banging. He eased to a halt, then stepped out into an atmosphere so unpleasantly thick and static filled that he had to gasp for breath. Raising the hood, he gasped again, this time in disbelief. For some reason, all the spark plugs were trying to fire at once, instead of in their usual precise sequence. He paid little attention to a noticeable roar passing to his south, assuming it was a train.

For more than 30 miles, the tornado had been hugging the ground after blasting through Glazier and Higgins. For the most part it chewed through nothing but dust and weedy vegetation and stunted trees. That changed shortly before nine o'clock. Out of the darkness, the maelstrom swooped in off the open prairie and made contact again with civilization, first at the unmanned United States Field Station at the southwestern edge of Woodward. Little escaped its embrace, now a fearsome 1.8 miles wide.

It sent sorghum grain seed spiraling miles high. It stomped flat a machinery shed. Trees popped out of the ground like dead weeds. Miles of barbed-wire fencing that it swallowed became a tangled, lacerating whip. It swept up sour-smelling moss and brackish water from the field station lake just before cresting a knoll. Below lay the massive grain elevators, softly winking lights, and neatly laid out streets of Woodward. At full strength, the tornado thundered down a hill toward Main Street and neighborhoods in the northwest.

At the Terry theater two children begged their parents to stay for the cartoon at the end of the movie. They were to see little of it. Mighty Mouse flashed on the screen, then the lights went out for good. Down the block, the skylight shattered at the Woodward theater and the awning tumbled down. At the telephone office the entire switchboard flared with light, and broken glass, roofing tar paper, and sections of awning crashed through the window. Then the switchboard went dark.

The noisy storm prompted Dr. Joe Duer to leave his seat in Gill's Cafe. Ordinarily a gruffly good-natured man, Duer was annoyed. He knew this storm was on its way, but his wife had insisted on dining out. Suddenly the frantic restaurant owner exclaimed, "My God, look at that barometer!" The pressure reading on the instrument had plummeted. Duer looked out the front window. A blazing river of chest-high fire seemed to be coursing down Main Street. Rocks, sheets of metal, and nails hit the pavement at such terrific speeds that they threw off cascading showers of sparks. He recognized a peculiar humming noise.

"Everybody get down, there's a tornado coming!" he yelled.

It had already arrived. Sheets of tin whipped off roofs. Windows flexed, then exploded into hundreds of stinging glass bullets. Heavy I-beams took flight with the ease of feathers; driverless cars backed up; signs rapped out a furious staccato of distress, then sailed away. Houses burst apart and crouched occupants were jerked out of their hiding places like rag dolls. Dirt tattooed their skin, and wood splinters sliced into their flesh. At 8:43 P.M., the storm decisively drew the curtain over its handiwork by severing electrical service everywhere with the demolition of the Oklahoma Gas and Electric plant.

At the Oasis steakhouse, the destruction began with tin

ripping off the roof and windows bulging crazily. A five-year-old girl said calmly to her grandmother, "It's time to die, isn't it?" Next to the jukebox, waitress Agnes Hutchison tried to hold shut the front door, then realized the futility. It was like trying to close a lone porthole on a sinking ship. At the cash register, amidst a lively flutter of loose receipts, the owner's wife cried for help. Then the building broke up and Agnes was thrown into a seething night as black as the bowels of a cave, except for the occasional glare of lightning.

The wind rushed her along. She looked around desperately for something to hold on to. She almost wedged her body in a gap between two parked cars, but feared being crushed. Skipped down the street, increasingly helpless, she at last came to a telephone pole. She wrapped her body around it just in time, just before the tornado caught up with her and pried her mouth and eyes wide open. The flesh of her face crawled, shifted, flattened, and contorted. She fought for breath, unable to see or scream. A deafening roar filled her ears.

When it was all over, when the enormous pressure faded and she could again breathe and hear, she found herself still hugging the pole. She was alive. An odd smell pricked at her nostrils, of musty attic dust and dirty wall plaster and moldy things that had lain too many years in an airless basement. It was the smell of death, she thought with a shudder. Lightning displayed all around her the new Woodward, a junkyard of endless acres of downed telephone poles, limp and twisted wires, loose bricks, broken planks, jagged puddles of glass.

She looked out and saw much too far, straight through the rows of houses that should have blocked her line of vision. Her heart quickened. By lightning flashes, she began to pick a path home. She could see well enough to advance 25 feet before having to pause and wait for another flash. Groping her way along, she touched bare skin.

"Help me, help me," a crawling naked man cried.

"Who's this?" she asked.

It was a neighbor. Dazed, she stumbled along with a growing dread. Thunder boomed, then light flooded the sky to reveal a bare house lot in front of her. She was home. Only the foundation was left, no sign of Olan or Roland or Jimmie Lee. Think, she commanded herself, where would they be? She scanned the ground for clues. Felled trees and debris pointed northeast.

A block away, in that direction, she found them lying in a grader ditch. Her elder son Roland was crying, begging for help. Jimmie Lee was unconscious, his pulse faint. Still, she knew the stories of soldiers miraculously saved in the war. Clinging to hope, she screamed at Olan to assist her with the boys. From his slack mouth came one last sound, a death gurgle, and then she knew she wasn't going to get her miracles after all. The top of his head was caved in.

A cold rain began to fall, soaking her muddied white uniform. She climbed over a fence for a mattress, with which she covered them. Then, shivering, she flagged down a car navigating streets choked with debris. Two men took Olan's body while she carried the children, one to an arm.

They drove to a house near the hospital where victims were being cared for. Agnes was deep in shock by the time she realized that Jimmie Lee, too, was dead. She stripped the wet clothes off her pudgy five year old and tenderly wrapped him up in a blanket. Slowly she carried him out to a pickup being loaded with the dead. This couldn't be real, she thought. She was about to place her son in the back of a truck to be hauled away like an animal carcass. She implored God to let her wake from this bleakest of nightmares.

As she laid her son down for the last time, a man asked for the blanket.

"The blanket's going to stay," she said. "You're not going to take the blanket."

"It won't do him any good," the man coaxed.

"I know it won't," she snapped, furious. "I'll pay for the damn blanket. The blanket stays."

The blanket did stay and the truck lurched away, its tailgate down and its grisly cargo bouncing in back.

All over town, the tornado had struck with the same brutal swiftness. Before it hit, Thelma Irwin was in the children's bedroom. Little Joe T. was still praying, in a beseeching, scared voice, but she wasn't looking at him. A window pane was bowing inward. She couldn't believe it could bend that far without breaking. Joe T. was increasingly frantic.

"Please momma, don't leave me in here, momma," he pleaded.

And then the straining window shattered. Flying glass cut her face and the wind knocked her to her knees. Blood trickled down her cheeks. She saw Raymond run in, clad in the long underwear he had gone to sleep in. He whisked away Joe T., who was screaming and jumping up and down on his bed mattress. Thelma pulled herself up by a bedpost and staggered over to Jennifer's crib. She reached in to gather up her daughter, then a delivery truck caromed off the house, smashing partway through the wall.

The wall and chimney flue spilled down on her shoulders in a hail of bricks and boards. When Raymond finally returned, the storm was gone, as were both his wife and daughter. He hurled aside debris piled high in the corner where Jennifer's crib had been. A neighbor pitched in, but they didn't uncover any sign of Thelma or Jennifer. Raymond was wondering if the twister had carried them off when he heard a faint noise in the rubble. Redoubling their efforts, the men found mother and daughter buried a good five feet deep in broken laths and plaster.

They were unconscious. Raymond took Thelma to the sleeping porch. Her eyes fluttered open briefly, long enough to see fires on the horizon that seemed to be burning everywhere. She begged for water. There was none, so Raymond used milk to wash her face and wet her lips. Her injuries were very bad, and Thelma passed out. Her next dim sensation was of being jostled about on the bed of a truck. Stiff, clammy bodies pressed against her on all sides. The truck braked.

"Who have you got there?" a woman called.

The man driving replied, "These people are all dead."

Dear God, I'm not dead, she thought. Oh, please God.

She had always drawn upon a reservoir of spiritual strength in difficult times. Her dying mother had extracted a promise from her husband that all 14 of their children would be church-going Christians. Thelma was only a baby then. Her father kept his word, assembling the children to read them the Bible in the evening. Thelma grew into a resilient young girl. The firm, resolute features of her face hinted at her inner fortitude. Once, kids shoved her off a huge straw mound onto ground beaten firm by cattle hooves. She had to crawl two and a half miles home with a broken back.

Thelma never gave up then, and she resolved once again to fight back. She silently asked God to care for her, unable to bear the thought of her children being raised by a stepmother, as she had been. It just wasn't the same.

Sometime later—she could not tell how much time had elapsed—she felt cool grass on her bare skin.

"Come here, doctor, come here quick," a woman cried out. "I don't believe this woman's dead."

Her eyelids were pried open. A flashlight beam stabbed painfully into her unblinking eyes. She still couldn't move, but the doctor saw a sign of life, however feeble. She was moved from the grass in front of the hospital, where dead bodies awaited identification, to the hard floor inside. Bobbing in and out of consciousness, she heard feet clicking briskly past her head and forced open her eyes. The tumult was unbelievable, a ceaseless stream of movement and babble of voices. With the sounds echoing through her mind, she passed out again.

The tornado had caught many people off guard, often as they tried to flee to underground shelters. In one astounding tale, a family raced outside to find their backyard storm cellar locked and bolted. As they were about to despair, a burst of high winds tore it open and they dove inside. Such luck, if this story can be believed, was unusual.

What happened to the Warriner family was more typical. John was still watching the ball lightning skitter down power lines when his father's voice rang out with a frightened urgency: "Get out of bed, get into the cellar, we've got a storm coming!" John and three of his siblings (the eldest son was downtown) clustered in fright by the back door, only feet from their root cellar. As Dorothy went to retrieve the baby, dishes in the kitchen cabinet rattled, then crashed to the floor. A moment later there was no escaping as the house disintegrated.

John blacked out, then became aware of something rolling him quickly over the ground. With each turn he felt handfuls of small rocks pelt his back. He blacked out again for a while, then noticed his father was calling to him from somewhere. It was dark, but quiet. There was a heavy timber lying on his left leg.

Soon rescuers arrived. They freed him and straightened his lower leg, which had gotten twisted up at an impossible angle against his hip. After loading John into a four-door Ford Model A, they drove him to the Woodward hospital. An aide came out to the car and directed a flashlight beam over the crushed leg.

"He's hurt too bad," the man said. "We can't do anything for him."

The Mooreland hospital, 10 miles east, was their best hope. The Model A stopped only one more time, at a service station where the men broke into a gas pump and worked it by hand to draw fuel for the journey.

Unknown to John, his mother and siblings wound up at the Woodward hospital after their ordeals. Only Leroy, one and a half years old, survived with barely a scratch. Dorothy had just taken him into her arms when the house began to break up. A flying object slammed into her stomach and paralyzed her. She fell and rolled across the floor, but never loosened her grip on Leroy. A collapsing wall pinned them and her chin came to rest on his throat. She prayed for him to be shifted so as not to accidentally choke him. He was, but into a position where his foot pressed so firmly on her leg that she wore a black bruise there for months.

Trapped under the wall, she felt his small body squirming. Dorothy whispered in a soothing voice, "Lay your little head down, honey, and go back to sleep." A neighbor who lifted the wall cried out, "Oh my God, he's dead." "No," Dorothy replied, "He's just asleep." Leroy started to cry and the neighbor grinned with relief.

Her husband Arthur was not so fortunate. She found him cold and shivering, begging for something warm. Dorothy grimaced. The crown and rear of his head were crushed, sagging back onto his shoulders. Spying a white cloth, what would forever be for her the purest, whitest cloth she had ever seen, she wrapped his broken skull. A funeral director later marveled at her careful touch. Not one drop of blood stained the bandage.

That she might need medical attention herself did not occur to Dorothy Warriner until the adrenalin surging through her wore off. Her spine was broken, and dozens of wooden splinters were buried in her body. At the Woodward hospital, doctors

proposed amputating one leg. Thinking of her children, she
refused. It was a small victory weighed against many losses. A
doctor glancing over her skinned, mud-covered face said,
"Woman, you're the blackest white person I've ever seen." He
didn't dare give her a mirror to look for herself.

Meanwhile, the Ford Model A speeding toward Mooreland
hugged the shoulder of the road to avoid a heavy flow of emergency vehicles screaming into Woodward. Stretched out on the
back seat, John Warriner groaned, the pain now throbbing wick-
edly in his left leg. At the hospital, he was carried inside on the
blood-soaked car seat.

As for the villain, the tornado, it was long gone. After slash-
ing through Woodward, it moved away to the northeast through
desolate ranch country marked by ravines and gypsum buttes. It
crossed the Cimarron River and damaged homes in Woods
County, but injuries were few and minor. The storm blew into
Whitehorse, then entered Kansas.

Some 40 miles north of the border, the last of the twisters
came out of its vicious spin at about 11 P.M., five hours after the
first one alit in White Deer. Vapor tatters hung in the air like
remnants of veils. These dissolved in the cool night and there
was no evidence in the sky that the tornado had ever existed. No
sinister wheel cloud pulsed down again. Nighttime cooling had
robbed the weakening storm of the pool of warm air it thrived on.
The fragile atmospheric balance had tipped. Finally, it was all
over.

Trailing the dying storm, the Siberian Express chugged
eastward. All the horror of this day had begun with this cold air
mass, unmoored from a distant continent to fly thousands of
miles toward a fateful convergence over the Texas Panhandle.
Tornadoes are rare, and violent ones extremely so, but the special set of conditions aligned perfectly in the atmosphere. It
produced a monster that had no face, but that was all swirling
body, kicking its way across three states.

Then, in perhaps the rudest turn of all, that monster was
gone, unanswerable for everything it had done.

4

Death and Uncertainty

The lashing winds had no sooner faded into the lightly wooded sand hills north of Woodward than dazed survivors struggled to make sense of what had happened. Some thought the tornado must have doubled back after reaching the North Canadian River and hit twice. Others assumed it struck a small area, maybe their house and a few others. At first no one had an inkling of the full extent of the disaster. In minutes, a twister nearly two miles wide had slashed through two hundred blocks on the north end.

Just moments earlier, it had been an ordinary Wednesday evening, a time to slip off one's shoes after a long day and glance over a newspaper, or page dreamily through a golf magazine, or embroider a lunch cloth. Now sobs and moans drifted through piles of rubble, as if this were a ruined city of lost souls. A close, choking smell of stale attics and wet plaster hung in the air. Retreating lightning strobed over a crazy kaleidoscope of images: mud-covered naked men and women sobbing and staggering through streets, crumpled cars with bodies inside, broken pipes gushing water, telephone poles bristling with rough beards of straw.

Turning to what was left of their homes, people dug with fingers or sticks. They worked by candles, flashlights, or lanterns, then a brightness lightened the sky. A grocery warehouse, hotel, and creamery were burning. An onset of torrential rain and light hail helped firemen suppress the blaze, but also poured into roofless houses and gave the night a raw edge.

On dirt streets, ankle-deep mud sucked at feet and tires, many of which headed to the hospital on Fourth Street. Dr. Joe Duer, after witnessing the river of flame light up Main Street, hurriedly left Gill's Cafe with his wife and daughter to check on their 11-year-old son, who had stayed home. Unfazed, the boy was eating cereal in the basement and reading by gaslight. Duer left for the hospital, a two-story crimson brick building. It was also undamaged. He bounded up the five wide concrete steps. Inside, two wings angled off the large lobby. Doctors busy treating a man with a skinned head peered across the candlelit room at him.

"You better get on the ball," he announced. "You're going to have more work than you know what to do with."

"You don't think it's that bad, do you?" a doctor asked.

"No, it just took off the northwest side of town," he replied tartly.

Then the door opened and in streamed the muddy wounded, limping and moaning. It was a parade of misery without end. The doctors quickly faced a crisis. Besides having to work by candle and flashlight, they had no running water or electricity. Bleeding could be stopped, but closing a dirty wound risked infection. They did what they could, patching with temporary bandages, splinting broken bones, and giving morphine shots.

After the 28 beds filled, people were laid on cots, on hallway floors, and even behind the reception desk. Hospital workers, too busy to remove dead bodies, shoved them under beds. Amid this chaos, a lawyer who volunteered to help got more than he bargained for.

"Get somebody to help and carry the dead people out," Duer snapped. "Put 'em on the lawn. Get 'em out of the way. Give us some room." The lawyer blanched, but began the distasteful task. On the front lawn there appeared anonymous rows of still figures covered by soggy sheets.

Looking around, Duer was reminded of serving in World War II, when he treated Marines at Iwo Jima and received a Purple Heart after he too was wounded and had to be carried out. Those memories still fresh, he seized the role of triage man, realizing that limited resources of manpower and medicine had to be allocated wisely and quickly. Some of the victims would not survive, others might. He kept decisions simple: give one patient a painkiller, transfuse blood plasma into another, send a girl with a broken leg on an ambulance to Oklahoma City, Mooreland, or Enid.

It was a depressing scene, even for a hardened war veteran like Duer. Unlike in wartime, these were not healthy, fit young men with single injuries, like a gunshot wound. As often as not, these were toddlers and the elderly with a multitude of cuts and blunt-force injuries. At every turn, he saw sad, hopeless cases. Children bristling with splinters like porcupines stared off dully into space. A plank driven between the legs of one woman penetrated all the way into her abdomen. She died.

A talented surgeon tackled the worst of the lot, the skull fractures, with the aid of Dr. Jacobson, the Woodward veterinarian who had been followed home by the tornado. It never caught him, but during dinner he heard a sound like a freight train full of junk passing by at full throttle, then saw fires burning across town. He decided to volunteer his services, believing the storm had claimed a dozen or so lives. It was much worse, he learned at the overcrowded hospital. Working alongside the surgeon, Jacobson picked out and pried up skull fragments to reduce pressure on the brain. In the end it didn't matter. Human heads were shattered like broken eggs. Not one of their dozen patients survived.

One man at the hospital who did live to tell a strange tale was George Devine. Before the tornado he figured that scraping together rent money due the next day was going to be his biggest worry. After mowing his lawn, Devine went inside, intending to retire early for the night. He and his wife Gertrude heard hail thud against the roof. When they looked out, it was calm. Too calm. Tree branches began to dance, then trunks leaned over in a gale-force wind.

They ran to the basement and huddled in a corner. Then George made an almost fatal mistake. To him, it seemed sensible to turn off the gas flame flickering under the hot water tank. He went over, put out the light, then returned to the corner. He began to slide back down into a crouch, his left arm gripping a foundation post. A board rocketed through the concrete-block foundation. It flew over the head of Gertrude, who was lying down, and crushed the bridge of George Devine's nose, knocked his eyeglasses across the basement, and sliced through his upraised arm.

Gertrude got up unhurt, except for a few nicks from jars of canned peaches that tumbled off a shelf and broke, spraying glass. George, however, was frozen in a semicrouch, impaled on the long plank that extended like a prong from the cellar wall. The jagged tip protruded through the flesh near his biceps, sticking out a good foot on the other side. Luckily its forward motion had stopped just short of a nail that could have torn up a major artery. In shock, but feeling no nerve damage, George slowly eased himself off the board.

Once freed, his left arm began to bleed heavily. Gertrude removed his tie and clumsily fashioned a tourniquet. She supported him as they climbed the staircase. On the top cellar step, they could see stars glittering. The roof was gone. They set out on foot toward the hospital, passing bare trees sheathed in metal from Quonset huts, then got a ride. At the hospital a doctor who shined a flashlight over George's white face looked doubtful. He had lost too much blood. Gertrude stayed at her husband's side and stubbornly held up a plasma bottle connected to an intravenous line. At last George was moved onto an operating table, where doctors stanched the bleeding. They wrapped a thick bandage around his arm and had him transferred to a 62-room hotel, one of many temporary care wards set up to handle the hundreds of victims.

Those in worse shape than Devine were dug out of the ruins all night, as loudspeakers mounted on trucks broadcast pleas for blood donors and searchers. In his 1942 Plymouth, Orlin Trego chauffeured a highway patrolman who had Trego stop at any knot of people gathered near a mound of rubble. The patrolman briskly advised the rescuers how to proceed, then the car sped off. Whenever he and Trego found a dead body, they stopped only long enough to tie a strip of white sheet onto a plank to mark the location.

Increasingly, the legacy of the tornado was death. At the Armstrong funeral home, director Franklin Stecher surveyed with a heavy heart the tornado's grim harvest, a series of bodies that had to be stacked like cordwood. At the hospital, some could be saved. At the mortuary, workers could only wipe away the mud from faces and hands and await identification. The disaster caused him to consider leaving a career he had never really chosen in the first place.

He was nine years old when his father, a poor country doctor, died. The family was left with little money. Stecher graduated from high school, too small to be a ranch hand and too poor to go to college. He could mow lawns, wash cars, sweep, dust, and answer telephones, so he got a job at a funeral home. Eventually he borrowed the money for schooling to become a licensed embalmer and funeral director. That expertise perhaps saved his life. In New Guinea during World War II he was an expert machine gunner, an assignment with a high mortality rate. After his superiors learned of his special skills, they ordered him to lay out a temporary cemetery on a mountainside plateau.

He never asked to do grave registration in the steamy jungle, shells exploding around him, but Stecher knew better than most that you don't always get to pick what you want out of life. He accepted that with a certain stoicism. In some ways, his past had better prepared him for tragedy. Even so, at times it amazed him what an awful toll the storm had taken. It seemed to touch everyone. An embalmer from out of town who was volunteering his services went to work, then asked if Stecher knew a Sam Schneider.

"Yes, and that's his son right there," Stecher replied.

"That's my nephew," the embalmer said quietly. "I'll take care of him next."

Out in the large funeral home garage, embalmers worked on makeshift tables arranged out of boxes used for shipping caskets. They cleaned away just enough mud from bodies to simplify identification. The dead were then dressed in long underwear and white socks, taken into the funeral home chapel, and laid on fence panels with sheets covering them up to their necks. As the embalmers went about their work, they couldn't help being bothered by the presence of so many children. One of the very youngest was two-month-old Paula Gayle Damron.

Like many, the Damrons had waited too long to seek shelter. Eldon, a 21-year-old press operator at a cheese factory, and his wife Eileen, 17, lived in a rented two-room apartment in her grandparents' house. The storm's approach made Eileen nervous. As a child, she had experienced a tornado. "Holler to grandma and let's get the baby and go to the basement," she urged Eldon. Unconvinced of the threat, he didn't even reply. By the time he realized his wife's instinct was right, they were trapped.

"We can't go out there, the porch is going," he said at the back door. Unable to hold it shut, he turned to hug his wife, who was clutching their baby daughter. The walls pulsed under increasing pressure, the lights went out, and a moment later the eastward-facing windows exploded inward. Eileen felt a tremendous weight crushing her hips. The heaviness lifted, then wind seemed to be blowing her everywhere at once.

She and Eldon landed 35 feet away, by a clothesline pole in the yard.

"Where's the baby?" Eldon asked.

"I have her," said Eileen, and looked down at where she had held Paula Gayle against her new white dress patterned with little blue flowers, which was now all dirty and torn. She didn't have her.

Eldon crawled around and pushed aside debris. Eileen's grandfather, frantic, his thick white hair tousled, ran out of the damaged house in his nightshirt, repeatedly asking if his wife was dead.

"Granddad, sit down, I can't find the baby and you're going to step on her if she's here," Eileen admonished. Without saying a word he ran away. Then Eldon spied Paula Gayle's limp, motionless dress. A rafter joist lay on her muddy head.

At the hospital their fears were confirmed by words of comfort that didn't come. A doctor with a flashlight examined their daughter. Paula Gayle didn't cry. He felt her head and turned to a nurse. "Wipe the dirt from her eyes and her nose," the physician said before moving on. The unspoken message was painful, but clear. Nothing could be done beyond restoring a little dignity.

Early the next morning, Paula Gayle was pronounced dead. Her parents were never able to attend her funeral because of the seriousness of their own injuries. Eileen's hips were sliced up so badly that when her filthy clothes were peeled off her cousin screamed at the sight. A doctor who tweezed countless splinters from her body quipped he should've saved them for her to build a house. When her hair was brushed for the first time, she lay down with her head above a newspaper. Cedar bark, glass, and moss spattered onto the pages.

Eldon had five broken ribs, according to an X-ray. A doctor ordered him taken to Oklahoma City, almost 150 miles away. Before the ambulance left, Eileen summoned members of their church to pray at his bedside. On the ride Eldon was well sedated, but near the end, a bump in the road caused sharp pain to shoot through his upper body. Oklahoma City doctors drained fluid from his chest, but were puzzled. He had a collapsed lung, but not a single broken rib.

The Damron story blended elements that were to become familiar: the odd selectivity of the tornado (Eileen was full of splinters, Eldon had none), the random cruelty that respected neither age nor sex, the disabling shock, the power a battered town found in prayer, and the confusion. During the recovery, a newspaper listed Eldon as dead. The mortuary had tagged Paula Gayle as "Eldon Damron's baby," and a rushed reporter omitted the last word.

Like Eldon Damron, many injured survivors were loaded onto one of the ambulances queued up at the Woodward hospital. Some were taken to Mooreland. The hospital there had been tidied up for a prestigious conference of doctors the following evening, then the tornado victims arrived and gurneys clattered over and scuffed the polished floors. Banquet treats disappeared from refrigerators to feed doctors, nurses, volunteers, and patients.

Even with so much sorrow and pain, there were light moments. Mooreland nurses found themselves smiling at comments made by spunky, candid children. A five-year-old girl had been rescued after crawling along with head injuries, falling asleep, then crawling some more. After this ordeal her worries were rather mundane. "Don't cut off my pigtails," she instructed. "I want to wear them to school next year, but my shoes got blowed away, and I won't have any to wear to school next year." Another girl who gave out her name repeatedly got cross when a new nurse asked for it.

"Well, I've told my name six times now," she complained, "and it looks like someone would get it pretty soon."

Back at the Woodward hospital, at 3 A.M. Joe Duer had a
moment to rest. He calculated that they had treated three hundred people in six hours. Conditions were improving. A portable
generator restored electrical power for the lights, and doctors
were driving in from miles around to spell their tired colleagues.
Duer asked a volunteer if she knew where the kitchen was. She
did. "Get your fanny down there and get some coffee up here for
us," he said with good humor. Another volunteer salvaged a
large box of rolls from a bakery with all of its windows blown out.

At the same hour, a TWA pilot flew over northwestern Oklahoma on his way to Kansas City. Moonlight illuminated boxcars
tipped over beside railroad tracks near the Texas border. Glazier
was gone, except for a highway filling station. Over Gage, his
earphones crackled with an appeal from below for 30 pounds of
tetanus antitoxin, 25 pounds of bacteria-fighting sulfa drugs, 10
pounds of blood-clotting thrombin, and "all the doctors and
nurses available." "There was so much smoke hanging over
Woodward, I couldn't see exactly what had happened there," he
said on landing in Kansas City, "but I could tell the damage was
enormous."

News of the disaster was spreading. Radio calls out of Woodward for assistance flooded the immediate area. On the outskirts
of town, an emergency telephone set was connected to an undamaged line by a local telephone wire chief. All the while, he
dodged lightning drawn to the downed wires and broken insula-
tors. In the wee hours of the morning, a reporter from the Associated Press borrowed the phone. By flashlight he dictated notes
and fragments of copy to his news desk, reporting 50 known
dead.

Few details about the damage were confirmed when the
morning edition of *The Daily Oklahoman* went to press. The
Oklahoman, a newspaper giant published in Oklahoma City,
splashed two briefs on the front page. They ran below the headline "Woodward Hard Hit by Tornado." A chilling quotation
presaged what was to come. "Half the town has been blown
away," said a highway patrolman. The other brief, seemingly
unconnected, described a killer tornado in the Texas Panhandle.

In the afternoon edition of the *Oklahoman*'s sister newspaper, the *Oklahoma City Times*, a more complete, horrifying

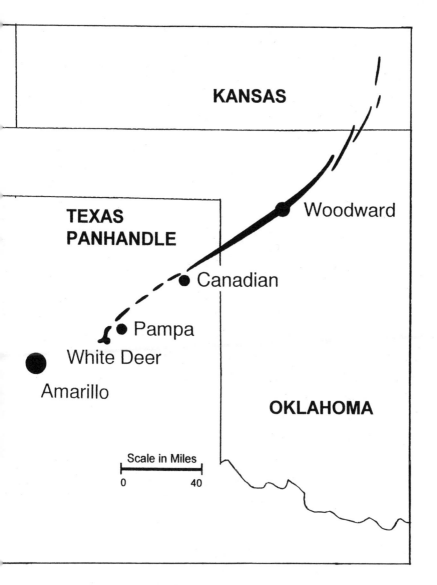

Path of the Woodward tornado, covering at least 98 miles. This recent diagram by a professional meteorologist reveals that the storm laid down at least six tornadoes along a 221-mile track. The dashed portion in the Texas Panhandle reflects uncertainty over path continuity there. *Donald Burgess*

Tornado at White Deer, Texas, near the end of its life cycle. This photo is one in a sequence that was taken by a traveling salesman. *Western History Collections / University of Oklahoma*

Warriner family in 1947, after the storm. From left: Charlie, Arthur, Maxine, Betty, John, Leroy, Dorothy. *Betty Nosler*

Agnes Hutchison with her two sons, from left, Jimmie Lee and Roland. Photo taken in May of 1946. *Agnes Giddens*

Terrific destruction by tornado of 220 blocks of Woodward, Okla.

Agnes Hutchison penned arrows on this postcard to show where, over three blocks, pieces of her house were scattered. Her mop was found in the black car, in the upper left of the photo. *Agnes Giddens*

Damage in Woodward. The Coca-Cola plant. *Plains Indians and Pioneers Museum/Woodward, Okla.*

Damage in Woodward. The assistant pastor of this church said,
"It looked strong with the brick veneer. But it just exploded."
Plains Indians and Pioneers Museum/Woodward, Okla.

Damage in Woodward. Aerial view. Note the sticklike appearance
of trees. *Plains Indians and Pioneers Museum/Woodward, Okla.*

Damage in Woodward. A tornado this strong can toss a car the length of a football field. *Plains Indians and Pioneers Museum/Woodward, Oklahoma*

A stone that today marks the grave of one of the three unclaimed girls. *Richard Bedard*

picture emerged. It was corroborated by graphic photographs published over the next few days. In aerial photos, Woodward resembled a European city bombed out during the war. Identification tags had to be inserted to pinpoint in the acres of rubble the remains of the grade school, lumberyard, and power plant. An *Oklahoman* reporter captured well the mood of this rude fall from grace, writing, "Once a laughing city of rodeos and lusty celebrations, Woodward lay crushed in sorrow Thursday after the darkest night and day of its history."

For such a sad day, April 10 dawned disarmingly bright and clear. Sunshine played over a landscape so bare that, for the first time in recent memory, the North Canadian River could be seen glimmering from downtown. The bridge was partly torn up. Steel windmills were twisted like corkscrews. Fur coats, bathtubs, and a car decorated leafless trees, as in a surrealistic painting. Branches, bent and twisted like swirly hairdos, pointed northeast to where the whirl had left town only hours before, as evidenced by clocks frozen at 8:43.

With no time for reflection, Woodward mobilized. A welter of sounds rang out in the crisp air. Shovels scraped into debris, displacing it a chunk at a time. Generators throbbed. A winch on a truck groaned, hauling a safe free of a wrecked building. Rifle cracks signaled the death of an injured cow or horse as trains full of patients bandaged with white seat covers clattered out of the depot. Bulldozers and graders cleared a path down Main Street for shrieking ambulances headed for the Army airfield a few miles west of town. There, the injured were loaded onto military C-54 and smaller C-47 transport planes and flown to Tinker Air Force Base near Oklahoma City.

Wading through the damage, people began to assess what they'd lost. Sometimes only a corner of a house was missing, rudely sheared, as if bitten off by a giant. One man found a strange car pointing up like a rocket in his devastated home. He jested to his neighbor, "Get your damn car out of my living room!" There was glass from broken windows ground up finer than sand, and on one floor, an open copy of *Gone with the Wind*.

Looters capitalized on the disorder by making off with everything from a boy's jungle tent hanging to dry on a clothesline to a woman's cherished embroidery. Of all his belongings, one boy recovered only his Easter basket. A thief was even seen brazenly driving around and loading ice boxes and refrigerators onto the back of a truck. Once the National Guardsmen arrived to seal off and patrol the stricken area, such incidents became rare, especially since anyone caught stealing was treated harshly. One offender spent 18 hours in jail, then was taken 15 miles out into the open country and told to start walking.

But overwhelmingly, kindness and selflessness prevailed. A rancher enjoyed telling the story of how he was approached at the Woodward hospital by a doctor and asked if he happened to have a bottle of whiskey. Sure, a whole case, he said. He lugged in the whiskey, and that was the last he saw of it. Then the rancher was recruited to give shots.

"Doc, I've never gave one of these in my life," he protested.

"How many cattle have you vaccinated?" he was asked.

"Thousands."

"There's not a bit of difference," the doctor assured him. "The rougher you treat 'em, the less it'll hurt."

Sure enough, the patients fussed when he tried to be gentle, but they barely winced when he jabbed in the needle. He was quite pleased with his improving technique until the doctor asked how many needles he had used. Embarrassed, the cattleman realized he was using the same one.

Health workers at a mobile lab also gave shots, as a precaution against typhoid fever from contaminated food and water. Instructions were widely distributed on how to boil and purify with bleach any city water used to wash dishes. Fresh drinking water was trucked in, along with medicine, tents, beds, mattresses, food, and tarpaulins to stretch over missing roofs. Red Cross workers collected clothing at their base of operations in the community center and handed out sandwiches and cups of steaming coffee.

Of all the relief workers, most memorable in their manner were the Mennonites, members of a religious sect known far and wide over the Great Plains for their aid after disasters. They had an aura of mystery and humble decency. Unasked, they climbed ladders to help shingle houses, then vanished without a word. They donated quilts that smelled so good, after the damp, dog-like odor that permeated clothes soaked in the storm, that one woman thought it must be the aroma of heaven itself.

Neighbor helped neighbor as well, and even striking telephone workers pitched in. In the hours after the storm, they worked all night by kerosene lantern to restore phone service. State union officials dashed off a telegram, sternly telling them this was no time to weaken. The return wire was defiantly incredulous: "Girls refuse to stop. Will work as long as needed. Have you seen this place?" The Woodward "girls" resigned from the National Federation of Telephone Workers and became local heroes.

A feeling of community solidarity was critical in the weeks to come, especially with so many dead to mourn. The first funeral was held Saturday morning, just three days after the tornado. In a bitterly cold rain, three unpaid grave diggers wearing rain gear provided by the Red Cross shoveled out a hole smaller than most. A Salvation Army official sang "Safe in the Arms of Jesus" as two plain wooden caskets were lowered into the wet earth. They were brothers, one four, the other two months old. Their graves received bright flower bouquets, compliments of Texas and Oklahoma florists. Not long after this simple ceremony, Elmwood Cemetery turned boggy and tractors had to pull hearses to their graveside destinations.

Sometimes the warmth of life persisted in the afterlife. Leon Schneider, 14, with his thin face, full lips, and dark pompadour, seemed to be asleep in his coffin, a nudge from waking up. Conscientious and hardworking, he had dreamed of being a preacher. He delivered newspapers with his white cocker spaniel on his bicycle handlebars. The dog refused to leave his side in death and went away forever after Leon was carried off. At the funeral, Boy Scout troop members were his pallbearers as his father wept uncontrollably. Sam Schneider was unable to stop blaming himself for not protecting his son from a falling wall.

At least Leon did not die anonymously, as was the strange destiny of three girls. No one knew, or would admit to knowing, who they were. One was about three years old with a distinctive scar on her left index finger. Viewers at the Armstrong funeral home affixed three different surnames to her. Funeral director Franklin Stecher figured he had this mystery solved. One belonged to her father, one to her remarried mother, and the last to the grandmother she actually lived with. Her blanket-wrapped body was shown to the grandmother, hospitalized with storm injuries. She wasn't sure, she said. Neither was the estranged father.

Nevertheless, funeral home officials felt certain of her identity—not so for the other two. The first, a baby girl probably less than a year old, was understandably tough to assign a name to because no one inquired for her. Over her short life, naturally she would have left behind few records of her existence. But the blonde . . . she was about 12, with severely chewed fingernails. Stecher had Woodward elementary school teachers file past her body, grade books in hand. Not one recognized her.

Some hypothesized that the unclaimed girls blew in from Texas, more than 35 miles away. Light objects did travel fantastic distances. An envelope landed 107 miles away, in Turon, Kansas. Even so, a quarter-ounce envelope possesses a much different weight and aerodynamics. A human is rarely carried even one mile in a tornado. A more plausible notion is that the girls' families were poor, or that they happened to be transients passing through.

The most riveting mystery centered around an adorable little four-and-a-half-year-old girl who was thought to be alive. Joan Gay Croft was a shy blue-eyed blonde with bangs and curls. She liked colorful hair bows and frilly dresses, and bashfully slipped behind her mother's dress in the presence of strangers. She pronounced her name "jo-gay." And she disappeared under very peculiar circumstances.

After the twister crashed through their home, Joan Gay and Jerry, her older half sister, were taken to the Woodward hospital with minor injuries. Joan Gay had a pencil-sized splinter jutting out of her left calf. The girls huddled under a blanket in the basement until their aunt Ruth Caruthers, looking for her own injured mother, heard that they were there. When she found them, Joan Gay and Jerry cried out for their mother Cleta. Caruthers held her tongue, unable to bring herself to tell them the truth. Cleta had been killed instantly and their father was badly injured. She promised to return in the morning. Sobbing, Joan Gay tried to toddle after her.

Caruthers accompanied her own mother to the Mooreland hospital. She was then drafted for nursing duties and cared for patients through the night. Early the next morning, she borrowed a doctor's car to go check on her nieces. She retraced her steps, but this time, Jerry was waiting alone in the hospital basement. A sketchy story came together, of two men in khaki outfits who asked the receptionist specifically for the Croft children, then carried Joan Gay on a stretcher outside to a waiting automobile.

"I don't want to leave my sister," Joan Gay had protested. They would return for Jerry, they promised. They never did.

There seemed to be no need to panic, considering all the tumult in the storm's aftermath. Joan Gay's relatives started making inquiries at area hospitals. No unidentified girl matched her description. They began to fear the worst. Stecher thought one of the unclaimed bodies might be her, so Caruthers sifted through a hamper of dirty clothes at what remained of the Croft house. She retrieved a pair of shoes, a dress, and underwear, all once worn by Joan Gay. Carrying these items into the mortuary, she steeled herself for a grim resolution. The clothing didn't fit though. The dress hung below the feet of one of the dead girls.

Determined not to abandon hope, Joan Gay's grandfather, Raymond Goble Sr., embarked on an exhaustive personal search. Goble, a former trucker with an ailing wife, traveled alone to nearby states. He posted fliers that asked the whereabouts of a girl, 3 feet 5, 42 pounds, chunky build, with chicken pox scars on her forearms. He placed missing person ads on radio stations and in newspapers. His quest ended only after his sudden death from a massive heart attack.

For decades, questions have swirled. Could the degree of Joan Gay's injuries have been underestimated? Was she a dead unknown? Or was she kidnaped by someone taking advantage of the chaos to acquire a blonde, blue-eyed daughter? Or was she sent to a hospital and somehow lost in the confusion? If she did surface in a fresh life, details from her past smudged by her abductors or adoptive parents, wouldn't she later have a dim memory of a traumatic night that might lead her, someday, to investigate who she really was?

Her story became part of the larger mystery surrounding the 1947 tornado. Oddities bordering on the supernatural became commonplace. Everyone knew of some unusual occurrence. Paul

Nelson, 13, never forgot two bits of strangeness. His mother always kept a plaid Indian blanket on the back seat of their brand new station wagon. The storm tore up the garage, but the car was pretty much okay except the blanket was missing. Closed up airtight, the station wagon had only one hole—the size of a baseball—in the windshield. And then there was the Brownie camera in his bedroom. The developed film revealed a blurry shot he never recalled taking. In the dark image protruded boards—part of a wall, maybe a rafter. Paul wondered if a tornado could take a picture of itself. Now that was an unsettling thought.

5

A Painful Recovery

It came to be known simply as "The Storm." Never did two words in this gritty prairie town convey so much. They released a flood of bitter memories and grief, and that grief sat cold in the heart for many years, even after trash no longer dotted tree tops and wounds slow to heal mended in knots of scar tissue. A small evergreen at the corner of the courthouse symbolized something about the new Woodward. The tree had held fast; it too was a survivor. But it now tilted eastward, forever to bear the imprint of what had happened one April night.

For weeks afterwards, a miasma of gloom hung over the town. Visitors, seeing the natives with their glazed eyes and unsmiling faces, thought this must be what zombies would look like, then pushed the unkind comparison from their minds. It was not an apt metaphor anyway. The blankness of expression on so many faces was not from an inability to suffer. Rather, it resulted from an all-too-human nature that suffered too much, and slipped into a sort of paralysis as a consequence.

Everyone was marked somehow. A 15-year-old girl kept hearing chilling screams in her nightmares. They were hers, she realized with a start. She was reliving being lofted in the air, as high as electrical lines on utility poles, all the while screaming helplessly. Having nightmares was more common than the reaction of an amateur pilot. He had just gotten his license before the storm and took his wife for an enjoyable hour-long flight that Easter Sunday, over sunny fields of ripening wheat. After April 9, and he never understood why, he never again desired to fly a plane.

Very young children were easily startled by loud, sudden noises, and acted insecure and nervous. A newspaper photo showed a girl, three years of age, being discharged from a hospital. A white caplike bandage encircled her head and sloped down to her eyebrows. At last doctors had removed a metal plate inserted to help mend her broken skull, but instead of joy at going home, her round blue eyes betrayed a deep anxiety. She clung fiercely to the nurse who held her.

Right after the disaster, the entire town was jittery about the weather. April was, after all, early in the storm season. The next prediction of thunderstorms for northwestern Oklahoma dominated conversation in shops and at breakfast tables. The Weather Bureau, following its policy at the time, never actually used the word "tornado." Nevertheless an Oklahoma City weatherman quoted in the newspaper judged conditions "tornadic." A tense day passed. No twister snaked out of the clouds, but all that spring people studied terse daily forecasts for any significant wording.

They knew weather could kill and had to be watched closely. George Goetzinger, a senior in the Woodward High School class of 1947, learned to beware of "eggs in clouds," or what meteorologists call mammatus clouds, which often portend severe weather. He also decided to disregard Indian legend. That fall, when he attended the Agricultural and Mechanical College in Stillwater, his Oklahoma classmates related virtually identical tales of how their town was protected from tornadoes by proximity to some hill or mountain. Misled once, Goetzinger thought, "That same damn Indian must have gone all over the country."

Superstition, Woodward knew, was no substitute for common sense and caution. No one took chances anymore. With hail pounding on the roof, a woman who lost her son to the tornado told her children that they were going out to the storm cellar. At her husband's objection, she snapped, "I lost one kid, I'm not losing another." Out they went, a washtub covering their heads. They slept the night underground. Another time, fearful of lightning, she ordered her daughter to remove the metal curlers from her hair.

Storm shelters surged in popularity. "Everyone was looking for 'fraidy holes,' looking for any open spot there was to dig a hole," one man later recalled. His grandfather even rigged a contraption to transport his wheelchair-bound wife to the cellar. Two boards laid over the stairs served as runners for the wheels. The grandfather decided the rope-and-pulley invention needed further refining after testing it out on his daughter, who plunged to a crash landing when he lost control of the hand crank.

Some people just chose to move. Frankie McCreary was riding west of Woodward in a carful of relatives with her baby son on her lap when her uncle, at the wheel, idly remarked, "Look at this rain. Have you ever seen rain like this?" It fell in slanted sheets. A storm was coming out of the southwest, and McCreary noticed shifting winds blowing hot, then cold. Sensing her fear, her uncle began talking to the car, coaxing it along: "C'mon old tin lizzie, we're going to make it." Near Fargo he said, "Look at that funny cloud." To the south a two-tailed funnel was sweeping across the ground. That did it. With her family, McCreary soon left Woodward.

That kind of action appeared irrational only to outsiders. Those caught in the storm's clutches knew how difficult recovery really was, behind the brave vows to rebuild. The damage was measured in scores of blocks and millions of dollars, but the recovery effort went at a painful creep, one day at a time. It was an ongoing process that meant more than houses being framed up for the newly homeless or a lace bark elm being planted to begin to replace the many American elms uprooted. It meant being able to cry again, or taking the first uncertain steps on an artificial leg.

Thelma Irwin knew both the sadness and physical pain. She survived being buried alive with her baby daughter, but at a great physical price. Her litany of injuries was unbelievable: a jaw, three ribs, and nose, all broken; a dislocated right arm; chipped teeth that had to be pulled; an elbow skinned raw; chunks of hair torn from her scalp. For days she saw nothing but dim light out of her right eye as tiny pieces of gravel worked themselves out. On an Enid hospital examining table, Thelma became an unwitting exhibit. Amazed doctors filed past to feel her arm. Neither skin nor bones were broken, but she was beaten up so badly that the flesh felt as malleable as raw hamburger.

During her recovery she dropped 20 pounds and new hair grew out like straw, which she interpreted as a barometer of her poor health. A friend who volunteered to brush out her snarled hair also smoothed out a ridge on her scalp by scrubbing it flat with a toothbrush. All the gravel and other junk that fell out was almost enough to fill a tea cup. For a long time, Thelma covered the bare patches of skin on her head by wearing knitted turbans and little hats.

Half a dozen families, including the Turkles of Wichita, Kansas, took turns caring for her. It was Alma Turkle to whom Thelma, the day of the tornado, had mailed the well-secured package containing the overalls—which reached Wichita, but choked with dirt, right down to the pockets of the pants. During her stay with the Turkles, Thelma drifted awake one morning with no pain. It was such a pleasant feeling that she lay there, not daring to open her eyes. A virtual symphony of clocks ticked around her in soothing rhythms. Of course, she thought joyfully, she was in heaven. All her illusions vanished with one slight movement of her body. The pain returned, as terrible as ever. Nothing had changed. She was exactly where she had fallen asleep, in a bedroom at the Turkle house that contained a clock collection.

When she improved enough, Thelma went home. There, nothing was the same. Sections of the house were rebuilt with mismatched boards. The Mother Goose window shade and her framed marriage license were gone (both eventually appeared, slightly buried in the backyard). Their cherished catalpa and cottonwood trees had been toppled. The clothesline had to be rehung for her at waist level because raising her arms hurt so much. Thelma never laughed during that unhappy time, even at the story of how Raymond was discreetly handed a pair of pants the night of the storm because he forgot to change out of the long underwear he went to sleep in.

The most heart-wrenching change was to her fair-skinned, blue-eyed baby daughter. After being injured Jennifer didn't regain consciousness for hours. Much later she was diagnosed as borderline retarded and suffered from a speech impediment. She grew up to be an outstanding babysitter, but died young of leukemia. In her grief, Thelma told others that when the river ran, it was with her tears.

One addition to their home lot that the Irwins insisted on was a storm cellar. A heavy metal bulkhead door opened onto wide steps, which led into a solid bunker. Thickly poured concrete slabs formed walls and a roof. Neighbors teased them about their underground fortress and called them cave dwellers, but during a bad thunderstorm the same neighbors clambered gratefully inside.

The Irwins just wanted to recapture an old feeling of security. So did waitress Agnes Hutchison. After the tornado, she plunged into severe shock, her sorrow bottled up inside her. She didn't cry at the funeral for Olan and little Jimmie Lee and wondered why others did. This was too awful, she told herself, and beyond tears. Death was forever, and inalterable. Her badly bruised face and body healed, but she only drank malts for nourishment because she couldn't swallow food past the lump in her throat.

She kept busy so as not to think. She salvaged lengths of two-by-fours from the rubble on her lot and erected a small house. It had stucco over chicken wire, simple electrical wiring, no plumbing, and a gable roof. After that she washed clothes for her eight-year-old son Roland, trying to scrub out the unpleasant odor that reminded her of the night of the tornado. Only after driving herself to exhaustion did sleep come easily. She had a new sleeping posture, with her body angled so her face was near an open window to detect a strong, shifting breeze. And so she labored to forget what she would always remember: that cold rain on her shoulders, an airless smell of death, the unbearable weight of a dead son in her arms.

Not until a few years had passed was she able to cry at last for everything she had lost. The tears fell during quiet moments, during times when she appeared outwardly calm, but her mind was sifting through images from that night. Alone, she sat and wept with a force that surprised and shamed her. Why cry about something that happened so long ago? she thought, scolding herself. Yet she did, and in so doing finally expressed a grief that had been locked tightly inside her.

In 1955, she had a new husband and four more children, and a home in Udall, Kansas. This time she saw the tornado on the horizon, wide and tall, a muddy wall of water shaped like a grain elevator. They all crouched in their old house, and the tornado roared in and tore off the walls, but the floor—and the family—stayed on the ground. Incredibly, no one was injured. Asked later if she had lost anything, Agnes said, "No." The refrigerator, washing machine, car, piano, and house were destroyed. But had she really lost anything? No. Not this time.

A dead child or parent was the worst loss to bear. A poignant news brief recounted how, after the storm, a son searched all over for his father. Tears welling, he approached an attendant at the Armstrong funeral home. "Do you have my Dad here?" he asked. He was directed to 55 unclaimed bodies, his father among them. "Now if I could only find my mother," he said, turning away. The young man was none other than Charlie Warriner, 17, the only member of the Warriner family absent when the tornado struck their house. He was downtown, out of danger. He immediately began a long search for his siblings and mother in several different hospitals, and for three restless days couldn't sleep.

At the Mooreland hospital was his brother John, whose leg had been trapped under a heavy timber. The dark-eyed 13 year old awoke a few days after his admittance to find himself in a four-bed ward occupied by youngsters like himself. One asked the doctor, "Where's the other set of toes on that boy?"

John glanced around. Two sets of pale toes stuck up at the end of all the sheets. He looked down the length of his own body. Five toes on the right . . . nothing on the left. The doctor ordered a nurse to give him a shot. He slipped into a foggy sleep before finding out his left leg had been amputated below the knee. By evening the sedative had worn off, but then a friend of his mother burst in and carelessly blurted, "Guess you know your Dad was killed." He got another shot.

At an Oklahoma City hospital his two sisters, Betty, 11, and Maxine, 6, were being cared for. Whenever the nurse moved her, Betty cried out and glared. An impatient nurse remarked that her younger sister didn't put up a fuss (unknown to Betty, Maxine was unconscious with a sliver of wood in her skull). An examination revealed the cause of Betty's surliness to be a glass chip in her back. It was removed. Nothing could be done for another source of anguish. She had retrograde amnesia. Her earliest memory was of lying in an airplane and hearing screams and moans echo around her, without cease. She would know of her father only through the stories of others.

The girls shared the same room. When Maxine revived, Betty was eager to help her little sister in any way possible. Maxine complained about the traction weights that kept her head raised all the time, and Betty had a pretty good idea what might fix that. She stole out of bed, lifted the suspended weights until her sister's head eased back onto the pillow, then nestled the offending objects at the foot of Maxine's bed. Her sister was relieved, but then the nurses scolded Betty. She persisted anyway until a doctor patiently explained that her actions were really harming Maxine.

At the Woodward hospital, Dorothy Warriner was content to rest her broken back until she heard that her brother was trying to have her children put up for adoption. Normally a sweet, gentle soul, she bridled with anger. She was determined not to let him succeed. She got the discharge she demanded, but only after being put in a steel-ribbed brace, like a corset, that laced up in back. If she fell, doctors warned, she would probably break her spine again. She would wear the uncomfortable support for eight years, removing it barely long enough to take baths.

Scarred but healing, the Warriner clan reunited at "Tornado Town," the Army barracks six miles west of Woodward that had been partitioned into apartments for the homeless. At the former officers club, they and 70 other families ate regular cafeteria meals on paper plates. "Tornado Town" wasn't a bad place. It had shiny new washing machines, a children's recreation room, a Red Cross doctor and nurse on duty around-the-clock, and a commuter bus service to Woodward.

But it wasn't home, and they were pleased to move back, even if that meant briefly encamping in a large tent in the backyard while waiting for their house to be rebuilt. Dorothy, at the age of 36, now headed the household. As soon as she was physically able, she took a late-night shift as a taxicab dispatcher for 25 cents an hour. When not at work, she caught up on household chores.

The Warriners scraped and scrimped and got by. Dorothy sewed the children's school shirts and dresses out of block-color cotton feed sacks. Chicken eggs that Betty lugged to the grocery store in a padded metal pail brought in a little money for bare necessities. Even with so little, the Warriner children found ways to amuse themselves. Betty and Maxine shared one red Easter sandal found in the ruins. They took turns gleefully hopping around the house wearing it.

Throughout it all, Dorothy governed with a generosity of spirit. When an addled rooster that had lost all its feathers in the tornado jumped up and clawed Betty's scarred back, Dorothy intervened to prevent a son from clubbing the bird with a baseball bat.

"You're not going to kill my rooster, after what he's been through," she said firmly. "He deserves to live."

John learned how to use crutches, but he wrote to the doctor who had removed his lower leg to find out why. In his reply, the doctor explained that gangrene had set in. Years later, in training to be an X-ray technician, John sometimes passed that doctor in the hallway of an Oklahoma City hospital. The man was always a bit reserved, perhaps sad. For his part, John didn't harbor any bitterness. He met squarely a new set of challenges and overcame them. Even on crutches he could outrun his sister Betty across a wheat field. He made light of his handicap. He propped up his bad leg on the family card table and pinched together loose skin on the stump, making smiley faces with the scar to amuse his brothers and sisters.

Behind this carefree facade he fretted over what would replace the missing end of his leg. He knew a man with a peg leg and worried about the mechanics of putting a shoe on a peg. After all, he vowed, he wasn't going to walk around with a wooden nub visible for all to see. An employee at a medical supply store allayed his fears by bringing out for his inspection not a peg leg, but a shapely, painted lower leg with a foot attached. John thought it was beautiful.

After he got his wooden limb, he flung the crutches in the corner and, despite the rarity of swearing in the Warriner household, exclaimed, "Dammit, I mean for you to stay there!" Whenever the cable snapped in his new leg, John had to wait for it to be repaired in Oklahoma City, and there were refittings as he grew, but he managed to ride a bicycle, square dance, hunt, and fish, all with only a trace of a limp. He quit high school football, not for physical reasons, but because the insensitive coach bragged about being the first in the state to coach a boy with a wooden leg. To John, it wasn't a wooden leg, but part of him. He saw no need to discuss it further.

His injury was the most dramatic in the Warriner family, but to this day others carry very real, physical reminders of what they endured. The sliver in Maxine's skull lies perilously close to her brain. Betty has a splinter near a major nerve in her leg (ashamed of her scarred body, she refused to own a bathing suit until after her marriage, and an examining doctor once asked who had shot her because of a tornado-related puncture scar over a rib). When Dorothy was hospitalized for congestive heart failure in 1993, she lost weight and a pouch on her leg was exposed. A doctor removed the cyst and sliced it open. It was a gritty time capsule filled with rust, dirt, and a decayed splinter of wood. "Tornado trash," the physician called it, like the knives, forks, and pieces of junk dug out of their yard topsoil for years.

One lesson of the Warriner story was that the human spirit could triumph, but not unmarked. John Warriner did almost everything he ever wanted to. Even waterskiing was nearly a success until he tumbled off a solo ski. In a school essay he composed six years after the tornado, he displays the compassion and tenacity that served him so well. He writes of the events of the storm and empathizes with a gypsy girl, who was about three years old and who lost her leg above the knee, an amputation worse than his. But he also reveals a flash of fatalistic despair as he refers to himself in a distant third person: "He is also known for his way of being so jolly and always looking forward instead of looking back on that time when he had two feet and legs of flesh instead of what is now and always will be."

"The Storm" ripped away childhood innocence, and this is not what appeared in any official statistics. As the numbers told the tale, damage along its path totaled $9.7 million, $6 million in Woodward alone. A Weather Bureau report estimated that the tornado traveled 42 miles an hour and injured 983 people in Texas and Oklahoma. Of the 169 people reported killed, 95 were from Woodward. The Woodward death toll was certainly higher, but is unclear today because of conflicting sources and unreliable newspaper lists. On a red granite memorial in a downtown park 103 names are inscribed. Donald Burgess, a distinguished meteorologist and native Oklahoman who has extensively studied the Woodward tornado, has verified that at least 107 people died.

Those who perished were not only the town's future, but a precious part of its past. In 1893, Mary Eliza (Miss Dolly) Kezer came to the small cattle-shipping town from Denver and sniffed about being a "ten-dollar woman in a two-dollar town." She became the first madam of Woodward's red-light district. Two sets of fine porcelain doorknobs, and her 97-year-old body, were dug out of the wreckage that had been her home.

Today she lies under a gravestone among many in a town cemetery that had to be expanded after April 9, 1947. Three simple headstones mark the resting places of girls never claimed, but not forgotten. Occasionally flowers mysteriously appear there. Legends on the stones of all the victims are terse, little more than dates book-ending a life. In August, when parched bluestem shivers in a hot breeze, the tornado that ended their lives seems impossibly remote. Then in spring, the storms return.

The Tornado
and Oklahoma

6

The Tornado

Tornadoes have been around for a long time, though not always under that name. The Oxford English Dictionary traces the origins of the word to the sixteenth century. In their sea logs, mariners reported being beset by "ternados," which were actually violent, gusty tropical storms. The OED speculates that "ternado" was probably a bad adaptation of "tronada" (or "thunderstorm" in Spanish). The "tornado" spelling refined and improved upon the sense by mixing in the Spanish "tornar," to turn.

What is perhaps the earliest preserved account of a tornado was recorded in a book better known for great plague and great flood, the Bible. In the Old Testament, a whirl snatched up the prophet Elijah about 600 B.C. In Ezekiel 1:4, the scene is described: "And I looked, and, behold, a whirlwind came out of the north, a great cloud, and a fire infolding itself, and a brightness was about it, and out of the midst thereof as the colour of amber, out of the midst of the fire." Its striking appearance was perhaps due to lightning and desert sand.

Etymology and early tales wind a route through Spain and the Middle East, but the undisputed home of the tornado is the American heartland. In fact the portentous catchphrase "Tornado Alley" describes a corridor that runs roughly north from north Texas through Oklahoma, Kansas, Nebraska, and then crooks east into Iowa. Within this turbulent region, central Oklahoma is a hot spot. It averages nine twisters a year over an area twice the size of Connecticut. Oklahoma City, a sizable target (the third largest city in land area in the United States), has been hit 32 times in 90 years.

Woodward learned firsthand of the geographical misfortune that plagues the Sooner State. Oklahoma happens to be about equidistant from the Gulf of Mexico and the Rocky Mountains, two large-scale features that influence weather. In Oklahoma skies, pitched battles are played out when dried-out air from polar regions streams over moist Gulf air.

The greater the contrast between the two air masses, the greater the potential trouble. Spring features the most marked contrasts. Wintry cold sometimes shoves out a sultry foretaste of summer. Probably native son Will Rogers had this season in mind when he quipped, "If you don't like Oklahoma weather, wait a minute." The jet stream snaking over the state during springtime plays a role by stirring up thunderstorms.

Still, there are garden-variety storms, severe storms, and tornadic storms. To make a tornado, a very special array of conditions must line up, rather like when a key hits all the right pins in a lock tumbler. Every year one hundred thousand storms are born over the United States, of which maybe 1 percent muster a tornado. And only one in five hundred tornadoes is comparable in strength to the one that struck Woodward.

To whip up such a monster, you might start with an unlikely setting, a scorching sun on a spring afternoon. The sky is blue, perhaps cloudless. Perhaps a car hums over a ribbon of narrow highway as a diamondback basks on a flat rock in a pasture and thirsty cattle jostle around a steel trough brimming with clear, cool water. It's hard to believe that in several hours rain will be carving channels in the ground.

But the appearance of calmness is the most superficial of illusions. A windmill twirls in a moist surface wind out of the southeast. A few thousand feet higher, the wind blows stronger, out of the south. Higher still, a faster wind rushes out of the southwest. Then, at 40,000 feet is the mightiest of them all, a narrow river of air known as a jet stream, roaring out of the west at 150 miles an hour. Vertically these crosscutting currents stack up like steps in a helical staircase, twisting around with height. These sudden directional shifts and speed increases represent strong wind shear—exactly what it takes to launch a storm core into rotation.

First, though, a thunderstorm has to boil up. Three distinct layers of air slide in to make this possible. On the bottom is a tongue of warm air. It has pushed up from the Gulf of Mexico, where it acquired moisture, a kind of yeast for the growth of storm clouds. The middle layer is warmer, and dry, having blown in from the southwest. Surging in over the Rocky Mountains comes the topmost layer, a blanket of polar air that is not only cold but dry. The tall Rockies have stripped from it moisture, which fell on their slopes as rain or snow. When mixed, these three layers will turn out to be a particularly explosive cocktail.

That mixing does not occur immediately. When parcels of sun-warmed air near the ground try to rise, they slam into the middle layer of warmer air. This abnormal capping feature is called an inversion (normally, close to the Earth's surface, air temperature decreases with height). The cap stifles cloud growth. Cumulus clouds leap up, crash into the ceiling, then subside and harmlessly flake apart. In the meantime the sun acts like a stove burner, pumping more and more heat into the ground layer of air. The inversion, like a stove pot lid, continues to suppress this boiling energy.

On this particular afternoon, that lid will not hold. Vertical circulation associated with the high-flying jet stream tears holes in it. At last clouds are free to grow. Warm, pent-up moisture converges on the holes and shoots up in the form of cloud towers. They are flattened and diced by rapid upper-level winds, but like waves of troops sent into a raging battle, others race in to take their place. Finally the energy cannot be dissipated. Bubbling towers pile up and ram like great white fists into the stratosphere eight miles above the surface, at speeds nearing one hundred miles an hour. This vigorous upward spurt creates a temporary, dome-shaped feature known as an overshooting top.

Heaps of burgeoning cloud matter have massed to form a cumulonimbus. In the world of clouds, it stands as a leviathan. Its very dimensions convey its power: 15 miles wide, 60,000 feet high (a commercial jet typically flies at 32,000 feet). Those in its path are forewarned of its approach by an anvil that spreads downstream for 40 miles or so, like a visor. Clustered on the underside of the anvil are row upon row of eerie-looking gray pouches, or mammatus. They can occasionally appear in startling shades of glowing green or orange, but are harmless.

A lightning flash officially graduates the cumulonimbus to the rank of thunderstorm. Lightning provides a natural release for tension between pools of opposite electrical charges. Most bolts arc back and forth within the cloud, but sometimes a stepped leader feeds earthward. On the ground pooled electrical charges rise to meet the descending leader. Then, some 70 feet above the earth, the two flows link in a blinding burst of light. In microseconds the lightning channel heats to 20,000 degrees, hotter than the surface of the sun. Gases expand violently, then a shock wave quickly breaks down into an acoustic wave—a loud crack and decaying grumble that is heard as thunder.

As the storm sizzles, hailstones the size of tennis balls thump into the wet soil. Hail is strange stuff. It sometimes feels soft enough to be squeezed like a sponge, at other times carries in its core such oddities as bacteria, fungi, grass blades, gravel, insects, fish, and even small live frogs. Reports of hail include the surely apocryphal, like a hailstone in India said to be the size of an elephant. The true record holder, at least in the United States, crashed into Coffeyville, Kansas, in 1970. It weighed one and three-quarter pounds, measured 17 inches around, and fell at 96 miles an hour, the speed of a fastball in the major leagues.

Hailstones flourish in a brutal environment. They are juggled by a vigorous updraft, the broad, rising column of air that sustains the storm. Hail starts out small and harmless, as a tiny ice pellet. Surrounding air is rich in supercooled water—droplets that remain liquid below water's normal freezing point. This water freezes onto the embryonic hailstone in coats. To grow large, hail must pull off a tricky balancing act, its rate of fall matched by the speed of the rapidly rising updraft. It bobs and fattens, then finally plummets at tremendous speeds, melting little on the way.

The blustering cumulonimbus streaks along, continuing to strengthen. Ordinary storm "cells" perish after 45 minutes. Towers spring up, become top heavy, then collapse in showers as the updraft changes to a rain-filled downdraft. But this storm is a supercell, a robust variety that lives up to six hours. Its longevity secret: High winds tilt the updraft into a shape that, if sketched, would look rather like the Leaning Tower of Pisa. Instead of falling straight down and stifling the updraft, waste products (rain) are thrown forward, out of the way. This kind of fierce storm thus behaves like an efficient engine, neatly partitioning intake from exhaust.

These internal dynamics are not visible, but before long, something breathtaking is. The central vault has taken on a sleek look, like cotton candy wadded around a stick. The updraft is slowly rotating, wrapping itself tighter. One theory of what kicks off this process draws on the idea of wind shear. If a wind current at the surface is 20 miles an hour and a crosscutting wind just above that is 40 miles an hour, for example, the speed difference causes a tubelike volume of air to roll. For simplification, imagine a fat pencil rolling over a table.

The rolling pencil is tilted up and swallowed by the updraft, which then goes into a vertical roll of sorts. The now spinning updraft takes on a new name, mesocyclone (for a medium-sized area of low pressure). Which direction it spins simply depends on where on the globe it happens to be. Air streams clockwise into a Southern Hemisphere low, counterclockwise into a Northern Hemisphere low.

As unseen mesocyclonic winds swirl and gather force, a revolving collar of cloud several miles wide pokes out below the low-hanging thunderstorm base. Below this feature, called a wall cloud, fingers of dark vapor twist and curl together, then break apart, then join again. A tornado is imminent. The broad, lazy rotation of the mesocyclone has tightened and quickened in doing so, in accordance with physical laws of motion. Consider a twirling Olympic skater. By pulling her arms in close to her body, she draws her weight into a smaller radius for a blurring finale to her routine. By the same principle, mesocyclonic winds that spin in a smaller circle increase in speed.

Then dust snaps up below the wall cloud. The signature funnel does not stretch down all the way yet, but by definition there is a tornado, an intensely rotating column of air on the ground. As it develops a very low-pressure core and rapidly pulls in air near the ground that spirals upward, the familiar funnel shape fills out in seconds. Small whirls look smooth and slender,

Prominent features of a supercell. *Joe Golden*

but large ones are ragged edged and unmistakably turbulent. This one expands until, like the Woodward tornado, it has a multiple-vortex structure.

Dirt and debris obscure the vortices, which swing around the center like dancers circling an invisible pole. These vortices are extremely unstable and violent. Passing over a wheat field they leave behind a peculiar pattern, a series of interlinked circles made up of junk hauled in by the tornado and then discarded. From a bird's eye view, these "suction marks" on the ground look like a huge wire spring, stretched and flattened.

North of a farmhouse, the twister demolishes a utility shed and a barn so swiftly that they appear to have been dynamited. It then issues forth a clacking roar. The sound made by a wide tornado has been compared to a cannon barrage, an amphibious tank, the roar of a thousand airplanes—or most commonly, a freight train. If narrow, it often hisses or buzzes with a sound that might bring to mind millions of buzzing bees, a mill whistle, or a giant blowtorch. Tornado noise, which has not been widely investigated by researchers, has at least three obvious sources: turbulence, the sound of objects like buildings breaking up, and interruptions of wind flow by ground obstacles (similar to what is heard when wind whistles through the trees).

The presence of irregular terrain such as a city or a hilly forest affects not only how much noise a tornado makes, but how it evolves. One idea holds that rough terrain disrupts the flow of warm air into the storm. In support of this theory, observers have noted that multiple-vortex tornadoes revert to a single-vortex structure upon hitting rugged ground. The waterspout, a less intense kind of whirl that forms typically over tropical waters, often breaks up after slamming into a cliff. Still, this variable should not be overemphasized. After all, during a super outbreak in April of 1974, a twister in Georgia climbed a 3,300-foot mountain, another in Alabama plunged down a 200-foot cliff, and another in Tennessee crossed a 100-foot-deep river canyon.

This particular tornado meets no such obstacles, yet it is near death. Despite its formidable appearance, it is a constantly changing flow, not a fixed object. Rotating winds drag a shroud of rain around the tornado, like a magician slowly encircling his cape to close out a show. The rain curtain blurs the outline of the funnel. Cool currents choke off the lifeline of warm, moist air. The storm has throttled its offspring. The journey on the wild winds is over.

Most tornadoes aren't as intense as this hypothetical creation. A typical one lasts a minute or two and sweeps out a path 50 yards wide and a mile long, while moving northeast at 30 miles an hour. Its winds clock in at 100 miles an hour. But with these storms, dabbling in averages does little to suggest the horrifying extremes.

For instance, a 1984 twister in Red Springs, North Carolina, spanned 2.5 miles in width. The Woodward tornado earned notoriety on two counts: it was 1.8 miles wide, and it tracked 98 miles. It should be noted that this track length is considerably scaled down from what was once believed, that one lone tornado covered all 221 miles. Meteorologists now know a "family" was to blame—multiple tornadoes generated by a single storm. After one dies a new family member touches down nearby, usually to the east.

What the extreme is for tornado wind speed, no one knows exactly. During the 1970s, finding this upper limit piqued the interest of the Nuclear Regulatory Commission. It wanted to design nuclear reactors sturdy enough to withstand winds so strong that they occur at a given location only once every 10 million years. Meteorologists today doubt that any tornado exceeds 300, maybe 330 miles an hour. This is reflected in the damage ranking on the F-scale, named for retired University of Chicago professor and noted storm researcher Ted Fujita. At the high end of the scale are F12 tornadoes turning at 738 miles an hour, the speed of sound at minus three degrees Celsius, but no storm on this planet has been classified as higher than F5 (all of the following wind speeds, by their very nature, are estimates):

At F0, 40 to 72 miles an hour, twigs and branches snap off trees. Some windows break.

An F1 tornado, 73 to 112 miles an hour, pushes moving cars off the road. It flips over mobile homes.

An F2, 113 to 157 miles an hour, uproots large trees and rips off the roofs of frame houses. The upper part of this range describes very strong hurricane winds.

An F3, 158 to 206 miles an hour, causes severe damage, lifting and throwing cars, overturning trains.

An F4, 207 to 260 miles an hour, is extremely powerful. It slings trees like javelins and levels well-built homes.

An F5, with winds 261 to 318 miles an hour, exhibits strength that can be described only as freakish. Trees are stripped clean of bark; solid-frame houses are whisked off foundations and hurled through the air. Cars soar more than three hundred feet.

Years after April of 1947, the White Deer tornado was rated F2, the one in Woodward F5. In the late 1940s, meteorologists who studied damage patterns in Woodward estimated the winds to have been as high as 450 miles an hour. No one at the time really knew what a force that intense could do, but amazing stories have long circulated about the mighty and strange powers of the tornado.

There are the strongman feats. On a May afternoon in 1931, a Minnesota tornado met an express train thundering along at 60 miles an hour. It picked up five 64-ton coaches and dropped one of them in a ditch 80 feet away. There was the Indiana twister that, like a child throwing a fit, tossed around 15-foot barn poles, driving one of them four feet into the ground. Strangest of all these events was what one man claimed to have witnessed. He described how a tornado snatched up a railroad locomotive and swung it about in midair, then set it down on a parallel track—facing in the wrong direction.

Not all feats require heavy objects to be memorable. In Nebraska, a bean was shot into an egg, leaving a neat, bulletlike hole piercing the shell. A prairie twister, after draining a pond, spewed out hundreds of frogs over a stunned town. A 1940 tornado in the Soviet Union swooped up a cache of old coins exposed by heavy rain and wound up scattering more than a thousand sixteenth-century kopecks around a small village.

Savagery and prankishness on scales large and small are expected, but perhaps the most perplexing behavior features an inexplicable, benevolent caprice: blankets sucked off otherwise undisturbed sleepers, harnesses yanked off unmolested horses. Some stories clearly stray into playful fancy, like the one about the sheep who continued to graze serenely after their wool was sheared. Other tales serve to awe and comfort us, of a crate of eggs carried four or five hundred yards without a single one breaking, or of a child who fluttered down after a three-mile flight, unhurt but for some scratches.

They enhance the storm's mythic reputation while softening its cruel edge. After the Woodward tornado, a story spread widely of a man in a car who flew over the courthouse, then landed safely. In the devastated town of Glazier, a filling station owner told newspaper reporters of taking an amazing journey over the treetops, then being lowered gently on his head, three hundred yards away in a wild plum thicket.

They're entertaining yarns and little more, according to Bob Davies-Jones of the National Severe Storms Laboratory in Norman, Oklahoma. He has devoted more than two decades to studying the dynamics of the tornado. He went on one field survey and acquired a dramatic souvenir for his work cubicle.

It's a frying pan, as thick as an old-fashioned iron skillet, that a tornado flung against a tree trunk. On the rim, a deep, scallop-shaped indentation hints at what really happens when winds take fragile human bodies for a ride.

"If they get carried aloft, as soon as the vertical wind drops, they're just going to fall to the ground, like a stone," Davies-Jones said bluntly. He knows of a man who reported flying in his car, then all of a sudden found himself driving across the outfield grass on a baseball field. No eyewitnesses ever stepped forward to corroborate that account. He can confirm an incident of flying steers in another storm: "But they were dead, 10, 12 feet up in a tree."

Scientific scrutiny has indeed debunked and demystified a number of claims and occurrences, such as the two visual cliches of strong tornadoes, straws embedded in trees and chickens plucked of feathers. Researchers have demonstrated, by firing a pneumatic gun in a laboratory, that a 145-mile-an-hour wind can sink a broom straw in a soft wood like pine or fir. In an actual tornado, lesser speeds may suffice because the wind apparently aids in this bizarre trick by prying open the tree grain. As for denuded chickens, their feathers loosen naturally as a response to extreme fright.

But sometimes, in places like Oklahoma, no one lets the truth get in the way of a good story. One classic genre freely peddles the incredible. Told with a straight face and a twinkle in the eye, the tall tale showcases not tragedy and terror, but comedy and confusion. The twister takes on the characteristics of a cartoonish icon and a mascot for a state battered by capricious weather. It possesses unbelievable strength, but like a Looney Tunes bundle of dynamite, explodes through stories and the imagination with bloodless force.

Here are some examples:

A man was rendering lard in a large kettle. He stirred it with his paddle. The wind whipped up and the sky grew ominous, so he ran to the storm cellar. When he dared to poke his head back above ground, his iron kettle was still on the fire. He fed the dying flame and resumed stirring, but with each pass the paddle clunked against something on the bottom. When he poured out the lard, he discovered that his paddle had been hitting the short kettle legs. The tornado turned the kettle inside out, without spilling so much as a drop of lard.

Or, what about the twister that crashed through a farm homestead and stripped ears of popcorn from their stalks. It shucked them, then shot the bared ears through knotholes in the old family barn. Friction heated the corn with predictable results. Kernels popped and fluffy popcorn piled higher and higher. Finally the barn exploded. The popcorn floated down upon a gathering of cows. Mistaking it for snow, they mooed, lay down, and froze to death.

Preposterous, but outlandishly entertaining, like the one about a man who was sitting before his fireplace before the storm hit. He came to 20 miles away, wearing a lady's nightgown. And in 1912, so goes one tale, a twister arrived in Stilwell just before a banker did to foreclose on a farm. The whirl tugged up the farmer's well and oil spurted forth. The farm was saved, the farmer made rich beyond belief. And then there was a mischievous wind that tore through a house in which a 10-pound bag of flour hung from a string in the kitchen. Afterwards the string remained, as did the flour—with no bag around it.

In Oklahoma, all varieties of stories abound, from tall tales and superman wind feats to an encounter in which a young man caught in a tornado was supposedly carried to safety by angels. It is easy to imagine this as a painting, the cherubs with goldbrushed wings bearing a limp figure. Maybe it would be called *Oklahoma Gothic*, for in a larger sense, this has always been twister country, this land where life was never passive, easy, or dull.

From the beginning weather asserted itself as a force to be reckoned with. Floods alternated with dry spells. Cold air chased out warm, never more suddenly than on November 11, 1911. At 3 P.M. the temperature stood at 83. By midnight, it had fallen to 17. A tall tale on this theme has it that, as a man worked his field with his team of horses in the blistering heat, one keeled over dead. As the farmer removed the harness, the wind shifted to the north and the other froze to death.

Even before pioneers knew about the moods of the weather here, they passed over the vast grasslands to continue west. They sought wide rivers and tall, sturdy trees, not trickling streams and small red cedars warped by the wind into arthritic shapes. When Oklahoma became a destination, not a stopover, it was not without event. There were ground-shaking land runs, the economic vicissitudes of oil booms and busts, and Dust Bowl days concurrent with a Great Depression.

In some ways, the tornado was just another obstacle to be overcome. More than one stubborn homeowner collected scattered boards after a storm and rebuilt, thereby contributing to the sense of a people willing itself into existence against the odds. A statue in downtown Oklahoma City expresses this indomitable spirit of optimism. A settler next to a thin, bowed horse drives a claim stake into the ground. "Passerby—" the inscription challenges, "look about and ask this question. Where else within a single life span has man built so mightily."

If the tornado fit as a symbol in the grand myth of Oklahoma, that distinction never altered its concrete historical existence as a feared killer. Woodward stood as one lesson among many. Snyder, 1905: 97 dead, hair reportedly stripped off dogs and cats, a roar audible 12 miles away. Blackwell, 1955: 25 lightning bolts a second crackling through the storm cloud, a glowing funnel, 20 dead. Gans, 1957: people swept from beds before a January dawn, holes carved in the ground 10 feet in diameter and 1½ feet deep, 10 dead.

Such terrible disasters send a strong message. Aside from all the talk of storm dynamics and F4s and featherless chickens, living in the heart of storm country really means being prepared for the worst. Yet Oklahomans don't pass springs in high anxiety. They don't have to. What may be the best tornado warning system in the world protects them. How it came about is an interesting story in itself.

7

Warnings and Weather Wars

BULLETIN — EBS ACTIVATION REQUESTED
TORNADO WARNING
NATIONAL WEATHER SERVICE OKLAHOMA CITY OK
433 PM CDT SUN MAY 07 1995

THE NATIONAL WEATHER SERVICE IN OKLAHOMA CITY
HAS ISSUED A TORNADO WARNING EFFECTIVE UNTIL
500 PM CDT FOR PEOPLE IN THE FOLLOWING COUNTIES

IN SOUTHEASTERN OKLAHOMA
    SOUTHEAST CARTER

INCLUDING THE FOLLOWING LOCATIONS
    ARDMORE . . . DICKSON . . . DURWOOD . . . GENE
    AUTRY . . . LONE GROVE AND OVERBROOK

AT 433 PM CDT A TORNADO WAS REPORTED IN COOKE
COUNTY OF NORTH TEXAS MOVING RAPIDLY
NORTHEAST AT 45 TO 50 MPH. THIS TORNADO WILL
CROSS INTO OKLAHOMA WEST OF MARIETTA NEAR
RUBOTTOM AND LEON . . . THEN TRACK NORTHEAST
TOWARD ARDMORE AND LAKE MURRAY.

PERSONS IN ARDMORE AND LAKE MURRAY TAKE COVER
NOW!!

In Oklahoma, more than 950 tornado sirens blend into neighborhood skylines, to stand in mute vigilance until needed. Oklahoma City alone has 38. There is nothing at all sweet or seductive about the siren song of the Sooner State. When the yellow flared head on the tall pole swings into motion, it shrieks at 102 ear-piercing decibels. Everyone within hearing range knows well enough to heed its shrill urgency.

The resemblance to an air raid siren is not accidental. The tornado strikes fast and hard, like a mad bomber, and takes no prisoners. No real lines of defense exist against such a natural disaster. No one prepares hours in advance by nailing plywood over windows or heaping sandbags on levees. About the best to hope for is a timely alarm, and a chance to escape.

Alerts come on two levels. The first, the tornado watch, takes the form of a box issued by government forecasters from one to seven hours in advance. It sprawls over 25,000 square miles. Within its borders, atmospheric conditions favor a touchdown, somewhere. At the next higher level of urgency, that somewhere is no longer a mystery. A tornado warning indicates one has been sighted by a spotter in the field or indicated by a radar under a distant dome.

Oklahoma averages 47 tornadoes a year, so warnings have to be very good, and they are. It seems unthinkable that these ferocious storms ever claimed one hundred lives in a fell swoop, as they did five or six decades ago. From 1916–53, they caused 230 deaths a year in the United States. In 1952, the federal government acted to stem the losses by issuing the first public tornado forecasts. As warnings sharpened, the death toll dipped. From 1953–68, it nearly halved, to 123 a year. From 1968–94, it fell sharply again, to 72 a year.

Today's warning system resembles the one in place at the time of the Woodward tornado no more than the Concorde does an early-model biplane. For one, local television stations now cover severe weather with the same intensity as breaking scandals and shootings. They broadcast flurries of bulletins that track supercell storms like escaped convicts. The dangerous whirl has thus been largely stripped of its lethal capacity for surprise. It is not at all uncommon for a TV weathercaster to detail a thorough projection of the path of a tornado, as if it were simply a city bus making scheduled stops.

Warning saturation is the rule today, unlike only a century ago. Not much was even known about tornadoes in 1854, when John Park Finley was born in Ann Arbor, Michigan. This son of a prosperous farmer was to prove himself a pioneer well before his time. As a young man he attended local public schools and colleges, then joined the United States Army Signal Corps, the branch of the army that controlled the fledgling United States weather service. Finley was an imposing figure, burly of build with a bushy, drooping mustache. His size was matched by an appetite for studying his favorite subject: tornadoes.

He hunted down records, some of them decades old, for an exhaustive report entitled, "The Character of 600 Tornadoes." He formed a countrywide network of spotters as well, which expanded to almost one thousand observers in 1884. These volunteers helped him piece together the details of a terrible 60-tornado outbreak on February 19 of that same year. Across the Southeast sliced a slew of twisters, more than 10 each in Alabama, Georgia, South Carolina, and North Carolina. The "Enigma Outbreak," as it came to be known, derived its name from uncertainty over the death toll, variously placed at between 182 and 1,200. The confusion arose in part because blacks were frequently not counted among the dead in the nineteenth-century South.

Improving public safety preoccupied Finley. He proposed that communities ring church and school bells for warnings. And, less than a month after the Enigma Outbreak, he embarked on an ambitious project: experimental tornado predictions. For his first efforts, he drew straight lines over a map of the eastern two-thirds of the country, dividing it into 18 districts. Each district he further subdivided into four sectors.

The challenge Finley posed for himself was simple. He would make a forecast for each of the 72 sectors. A handful of guidelines influenced his judgments. For instance, he knew that tornadoes often develop in the southeastern region of a broad area of low-pressure air. Finley went to work, and after a few months, he had a 96 percent success rate. That impressive figure was misleading, however. He credited himself equally with success for occurrences and nonoccurrences. In other words, for any day he predicted no tornadoes anywhere and there were none, he scored that as 100 percent accuracy.

Even discounting for this, Finley was doing a good job of forecasting. His superiors responded by promoting him to second lieutenant, and he was allowed to issue a disguised forecast of sorts. Instead of using the word "tornado," a special advisory would be sent out warning of violent local storms. For a brief time in 1886 he was allowed to use the forbidden word. Little did he know then, he was at the zenith of his career. His spotter network swelled to 2,400 people, then he took a tumble.

In 1889, Finley was ousted as chief tornado spokesman for the Army Signal Corps. His military career had been controversial, and a complaint accused him of abusing enlisted men. Without Finley, weather service officials retreated to a cautious stance. They feared tornado forecasts would just induce public panic and worried that they lacked the knowledge to make predictions for small enough areas.

That meant a flat-out ban on the word "tornado" in forecasts. The repercussions of that tentative policy rippled outward. Thunderstorm research suffered well into the twentieth century. For two decades the Weather Bureau didn't even have a central department collecting severe storm reports. Every so often during this long, fallow period, the agency discovered what a high price silence carried.

So it was on March 18, 1925. During the gay era of flappers and jazz known as the Roaring Twenties, a different roar was forever imprinted on the minds of thousands of Midwesterners. In southern Missouri that morning, drizzle fell in a dark gloom. No wind stirred the heavy air, then the skies split like overripe fruit, gushing rain.

Shortly after noon the twister began lunging over Missouri hills one hundred miles south of St. Louis. It whipped through rugged coal country on a northeastern track, leaving behind unbelievable devastation. The Tri-State Tornado (it crossed parts of Missouri, Illinois, and Indiana) managed to set several records that stand to this day. Its forward speed was as fast as 73 miles an hour, and it killed 695 people. Whether it was really one tornado or several, as later researchers speculated, mattered little to those in the 219-mile-long path of destruction.

The Weather Bureau parroted policy in its report on the disaster: no tornado forecast was made for March 18. But the summary also made a troubling observation. The pattern of the daily weather map's isobars, or whorled lines of atmospheric pressure, looked familiar. They resembled those from February 19, 1884—the day of the deadly Enigma Outbreak. Despite this tacit indictment of inaction, the weather agency didn't immediately strike down its prohibition on tornado forecasting. Rather, certain events and advances over the years conspired to lift the ban.

To start with, meteorologists found ways to gather the comprehensive data needed to make these tricky forecasts. For one, they began to fly their measuring tools into the sky, at first crudely with kites at the turn of the twentieth century. Airborne thermometers, barometers, and hygrometers could answer a hugely important question: At different heights, what did the upper atmosphere look like? After all, ground stations sampled only the lowest 30 feet or so of an active, restless, 40,000-foot-high troposphere. By the 1940s, the weather service had committed itself to scheduled daily releases of instrumented helium balloons called radiosondes. As they ascended, they beamed down their findings.

Just as critical as collecting more comprehensive data was knowing how to interpret it. That became especially imperative to the military after a costly disaster at Tinker Air Force Base near Oklahoma City in March of 1948. A twister blasted through unsheltered planes, and damage topped ten million dollars. The Air Force brass was rudely awakened to the fact that, out in the middle of Tornado Alley, its expensive planes were often left sitting in the open like ten pins. It happened that two Tinker meteorologists were already at work on forecasting methods for severe thunderstorms and tornadoes, to allow valuable property to be shuttled into bombproof warehouses. The officers—Major E.J. Fawbush and Captain Robert Miller—were told to put their research to the test immediately. They did. Only five days later, they sounded an alert well in advance of another tornado that slammed into the base.

Fawbush and Miller proceeded to circulate their experimental predictions to Air Force weather offices. When news of this leaked out, the public demanded forewarnings as well. There was a genuine hunger for such information, and resentment

about its being withheld. The story of the World War II secret
weather observer networks demonstrated as much. The federal
government set them up within a 35-mile radius of munitions
plants, at first simply to relay warnings of approaching storms (a
direct lightning hit could have triggered a cataclysmic explosion).
The weather service then quietly collected from the observers
tornado and hail reports too. Before long the public knew of the
network's covert operations, and insisted on being notified as
well.

In 1952, nine years after the death of John Park Finley, the
Weather Bureau finally threw aside its long-standing reserva-
tions and issued the first public tornado forecasts. Happily, the
skeptics within the agency were shown to be wrong. There were
no stampedes or episodes of mass hysteria, and only a few isolated cases of extreme panic.

Forecasting was only one element of a good warning system,
however. It needed to be balanced by minute-to-minute scrutiny
of any rogue storm cell that flared up. For this task, World War
II–vintage radars fit the bill perfectly. Like an X-ray machine,
they bared a thunderstorm's inner workings and structure. They
outlined areas of rain and hail, and their intensity. With time,
radar operators were excited to discover an intriguing clue on
their screens. Tornadoes sometimes spun at the tip of a curled
finger of precipitation. This telltale signature they called a "hook
echo."

Meteorologists eventually acquired other resources to monitor severe storms on the loose. The first weather satellite assumed orbit in 1960, and with its far-sighted overhead view,
discerned the movement of massive fronts and the popcorn
growth of thunderstorm clusters. On the ground, the SKYWARN
network of volunteer spotters was formed in 1969. It proved once
again that, no matter how superior the technology, the warning
system depended heavily on the trained observer in the field.

The acknowledged weak link in the system was at the point
of dissemination. An alert had to be put in front of tens of thousands of people, and quickly. The weather service had no avenue
by which to reach a large popular audience, in seconds, on its
own. To surmount this obstacle, it forged a partnership with the
broadcast media. When the teleprinter dinged in any Oklahoma

news studio, television and radio anchors scooped up the bulletins and promptly delivered them to huge audiences. Hence the weather agency managed to get out its messages, and each station burnished its image by being a source of breaking weather news. It was an ideal symbiotic relationship. Then in the 1970s, a maverick weathercaster decided to go his own way.

Gary England joined KWTV 9 in Oklahoma City in 1972. He was about as true-blue Oklahoma as anyone, a product of a small town in the northwest who knew how to raise a pig and drop lines for channel catfish. England won over viewers with a natural, self-effacing charm. His freewheeling on-air style belied the fact that he was actually shrewd, scrappy, and devoted to his craft. And to hear England tell it, he was embarrassed to be delivering tardy weather service tornado warnings. As he put it, "You could warn Henry down the street, but only if John's house blew away first."

One problem was technological. The standard weather service radar saw only half the picture when it looked at a thunderstorm. It picked out sectors of drizzle and shafts of drenching rain, but reported nothing about the motion of winds. England knew quite well that a radar capable of sensing both precipitation and wind movement wasn't a pipe dream. Just a short jaunt down the interstate, at the National Severe Storms Laboratory, researchers were developing something called Doppler radar. It took its name from Austrian physicist Christian Doppler and the well-known principle he discovered. The Doppler effect is often illustrated with the example of an observer at a railroad station. An express train nears. As it approaches, the observer notices a shift in pitch of its blowing whistle. The sound grows keener and higher. The pitch then lowers steadily after the train passes and recedes.

This basic concept has sophisticated applications, especially for radar. It works with wind—or not wind exactly, but tiny windborne particles, like rain, dust, or even insects. A typical Doppler radar first flings a train of microwaves 10 centimeters long. They spread out in an expanding cone. After they bounce back off moving rain and other particles, the radar measures the shift in frequency. A computer running complex algorithms then crunches the raw data. It draws an image of the storm as a giant wind field of tiny color-coded blocks. Adjacent blocks indicating fast movement in opposite directions show a possible meso-cyclone, the tornado precursor.

England avidly followed news of Doppler research at NSSL, convinced that this new radar would revolutionize severe storm coverage. He wanted one, but it wasn't the kind of item sitting on a shelf in a factory warehouse. With the backing of the station's owner, he had to beg an engineer at an Alabama radar-building firm to make him a small Doppler for a few hundred thousand dollars. The machine arrived, May 14, 1981, serial number 0001. With its big start-up lever on the side, it looked a bit like something out of a cheap science fiction thriller. Gary England didn't care. He could now boast that KWTV owned the first Doppler radar in the country devoted to public warnings, beating out the National Weather Service (the former Weather Bureau, renamed in 1970).

Yet he soon reconsidered the wisdom of what he had done. The first Doppler readout was unlike anything he had ever seen: a mess, digitized scrambled eggs. With no instructor to turn to, he took it upon himself to study NSSL Doppler manuals and reports. The fog of confusion gradually began to lift. The very next spring, when he spotted what looked like a dangerous wind signature, he rushed onto the air to alert the town of Ada. An hour later a tornado dipped down and demolished a trailer park, killing one person.

While England may have saved scores of lives, he lost the respect of local National Weather Service officials when he proudly noted on the air that his warning had beaten theirs by 15 minutes. He had upset the cozy relationship between the broadcast media and the weather agency. He wasn't content to be a government mouthpiece; he was aggressively making his own tornado warnings.

It was into this fractured relationship that Ken Crawford entered when, in July of 1982, he became the new manager for all the Oklahoma weather service offices. He brought to the job a strong background that ranged from academics and research to marine forecasting while stationed in New Orleans. The Oklahoma operation, Crawford was dismayed to find, was adrift. It lacked vision and ambition in the managerial ranks. Moreover, a little prying on his part exposed unhappiness among weather service "customers"—civil defense officials and media broadcasters. Beyond the polite smiles and cordial handshakes was discontent. They groused that the weather service played no significant role in warning the public. Its bulletins were too late and not accurate enough. Crawford realized he had to earn back their faith.

There was a certain absurdity to all of this, in the middle of central Oklahoma, where some of the most brilliant meteorologists were dedicating their careers to studying causes of severe weather. But reaping the fruits of their research wasn't so easy. In general, bureaucratic and political realities had a way of hampering progress. Such was the case with Doppler radar. Crawford, from having worked on the early stages of the Doppler project at the National Severe Storms Laboratory, knew the importance of a hot new program called NEXt Generation Weather RADar. In 1982, NEXRAD was on the drawing board, with plans to install more than 150 Dopplers in weather service offices across the country. Even so, he didn't expect his Oklahoma City office to get one of the powerful radars anytime soon.

"You could integrate it into one office pretty fast. But when you look at 50 states, and you look at the amount of dollars for NEXRAD going through the United States Congress, and you look at a decade like the 1980s when the philosophy was less government, there was no major push from on high to see this thing through. If it was a good idea, they thought, let the private sector do it."

As leaders in the federal government dithered over the future and funding of NEXRAD, a free-for-all broke out in Oklahoma. Every broadcast media outlet seemed to be generating its own warnings, with Gary England at the front of the pack. In 1983 Crawford counted six radars at television stations and four at radio stations. He watched in helpless frustration as bulletins of all kinds flooded the airwaves. When civil defense workers called the weather service to ask about the tornado warning heard out of Ardmore, the forecasters on duty could only shrug. In one extreme example, a disk jockey brashly told listeners during a bad storm, "The National Weather Service seems to be dragging its feet on this one. I am going ahead and issuing a tornado warning." This chaos Crawford later identified as the onset of what came to be known widely as the television "weather wars." He defined three characteristics of these wars: open criticism of the weather service, a competitive broadcast environment for weather, and abundant warning sources.

In the end, Crawford did win the better part of the battle. He helped revitalize the Oklahoma weather service. His employees began to actively seek "ground truth" data to match their forecasts against what really happened, to see how well they were doing. They tried out promising new radar upgrades and computer algorithms. Workshops were held for members of the broadcast media to improve relations and showcase the skills of government forecasters. By 1987, the Oklahoma City office's skill scores (a set of what might be considered batting averages for accuracy in storm warnings) were so outstanding that his peers thought he must be doctoring the numbers.

The disenchanted customers of the weather agency returned to the fold. Crawford took comfort in that, but realized that the genie was out of the bottle. The weather wars were here to stay.

8

A Saturday with Gary England

In spring in Oklahoma, the atmosphere works its mischief in accordance with no man's schedule. Television weathermen learn to tailor their lives to its vagaries. That's the way it has to be, and early on a Saturday afternoon in late May, Gary England settles in for what could be a long, long day. A feature known as a dryline, which frequently aids in kicking up nasty storms, is advancing from the west. Waiting to be plowed up in its path is a thick blanket of unstable, damp air. This recipe for trouble has produced nothing menacing yet, but England—a friendly, avuncular sort with a trim wrestler's build and twinkling blue eyes—doesn't intend to be ambushed.

He is keeping tabs on the changing skies from a dim, cramped room jammed behind a wall of the Newsline 9 studio set. From this cubbyhole in Oklahoma City, he can use his electronic equipment to peer into thousands and thousands of square miles of atmosphere all over the state. Fittingly, the room resembles a security guard's high-tech watch post. Wall panels hold row upon row of snooping monitors: a lightning detection network shows clustered dots flickering like swarming fireflies; a camera mounted high on the station transmission tower spies foaming piles of cloud on the horizon; a Doppler radar throws its beam all the way into Texas.

Returns on radar look "real flaky," England reports to his backup Alan Mitchell. For the moment Oklahoma is safe. Executive vice president Jerry Dalrymple has wandered in and, since no thunderheads are massed on the border, the conversation lazily meanders for a while. Then someone mentions "weather wars" and the tone turns ugly. The weather wars. The new ratings battleground. Each local television station wants to establish itself—at seemingly any cost—as the leader in zipping out fast, accurate warnings. They all buy the newest gadgetry and latest storm-tracking software, and send waves of employees toting video cameras all over the state at the slightest sign of rocky weather.

"It's gone beyond good judgment and common sense," England says, shaking his head.

Dalrymple, a pugnacious-looking man with dark, watchful eyes, casts the matter in a more cynical light. "Gimme sleaze, we can tease," he scoffs. "Blow it up news, blow it up weather. Flash and crash and trash."

There's a night scope, a new device being promoted like crazy by a competitor station seeking an edge. Apparently it concentrates scarce natural light, so operators can make out wall clouds and funnels in the dark. Through a night scope, a harmless dangling cloud evidently can look like Armageddon knifing down from the heavens. Everyone laughs derisively. A pause. Of course KWTV has one.

"We bought a night scope," Dalrymple grumbles, "because they were hyping the hell out of theirs. You feel like you've got to have one. We never use the damn thing."

What really has riled up everyone is not a night scope, though, but an error in judgment only weeks old. Dalrymple has the evidence. He slips a videotape into a player. May 8, 1993, thunderstorms hammering the state, the Oklahoma City metro region flooding, and on KFOR 4 . . . well, it's like a living nightmare. At the dead center of a still graphic is a dot representing the southern border town of Ryan. The two agitated voices talking are weathercaster Mike Morgan in Oklahoma City and storm chaser Jeff Piotrowski in Ryan.

PIOTROWSKI: (jabbering) Tornado coming right in, at downtown Ryan . . . tornado continuing. We're looking at debris in the air, Mike. It has hit houses now on the west side of Ryan. Houses are now exploding. It's heading northeast, Mike, heading east-northeast, Mike, into downtown Ryan.

MORGAN: Okay, Jeff, now where are you from downtown Ryan?

PIOTROWSKI: I'm in downtown Ryan, Mike. Tornado is one block west of downtown.

MORGAN: You people in Ryan, you're in big-time danger . . .

PIOTROWSKI: I'm now heading east out of downtown Ryan . . . the tornado continues on the west side.

Dalrymple interjects acidly, "This makes *The War of the Worlds* look like a poor man's production." The videotape jumpcuts to a news package with a reporter for KWTV 9 cruising through Ryan a day or two later. No tornado ever hit town, claims the police chief. More digging turns up a man who declares that not a single tree limb was blown down. To clarify, tornadoes did whirl *near* town. But this scene of a Ryan twister blasting away houses was pure fiction.

The humiliating public exposé then drew a spirited rebuttal from Channel 4, and an unpleasant spat ensued between the two giants. What Channel 9 did violated unwritten rules of local news etiquette. Stations just aren't supposed to air each other's dirty laundry. Viewers trying to sort all this out were left with several possible interpretations. One, KWTV made a principled, long-overdue stand against excesses and sensationalism in weather coverage. Or, two, KFOR made an honest blunder in the heat of the moment while trying to relay breaking news.

All that aside, no one disputes the fact that when a tornado does curl out of a cloud, you better be there if you want to be a player in this market. England starts out by coding the danger early. A Priority One day is a full alert. He dispatches five to ten crews to track various storms, and on occasion even raids the marketing department for bodies. The day's bill for overtime, vehicle wear, fuel, cellular phone charges, and satellite time for uplink trucks in the field will easily top four thousand dollars.

Stations pay because weather leads the local news lineup on many a night. Each year has its unpleasant surprises. In one day in 1993, seven inches of torrential rain transform the mild creeks of southern Oklahoma City into perilous whitewater. Several people die in the flooding, and all across the state, high water shuts down highways. Less than a month later, hail as large as baseballs reduces to stubble 130,000 acres of hard red winter

Cumulonimbus, not yet fully mature. *Keith Brewster*

Mammatus clouds. *National Severe Storms Laboratory*

A classic tornado shape. *National Severe Storms Laboratory*

Union City, Okla., on May 24, 1973. Tornadoes often appear white when viewed from the south or west. A team of research meteorologists was able to observe and film the evolution of this one. *National Severe Storms Laboratory*

Wall cloud. *National Severe Storms Laboratory*

As the tornado on the left dies, a new one could very well touch down from the hanging wall cloud on the right. *National Severe Storms Laboratory*

Enid, Okla., on June 5, 1966. The tornado was 100 yards wide and tracked eight miles, but its winds probably didn't exceed 160 miles an hour. It damaged more than 100 houses, knocked over four railroad boxcars, and injured six people. *National Severe Storms Laboratory*

One of 13 tornadoes that struck on April 10, 1975, as part of the Red River Outbreak (three of them crossed this watery boundary that separates Oklahoma and Texas). *National Severe Storms Laboratory*

This huge multiple-vortex tornado near Binger, Okla., two-thirds of a mile wide, may have been spinning 260 miles an hour. It flung about cars and combines with equal ease. *National Severe Storms Laboratory*

wheat up in the north-central part of the state. And that same spring a twister blasts through Catoosa, killing seven.

It's a very crazy scene out there. England knows this well, as someone who has passed along hundreds of tornado warnings. He uses the same stock advice, repeating it like a mantra: "Lowest level, smallest room, lowest part." That often leads to the first-floor bathtub, where people climb in, swaddled in blankets. Bathrooms have a reputation for surviving well, sometimes standing when the rest of the house lies in a shambles. But in a mile-wide F4 or F5 tornado . . . England shrugs, like a weary doctor assigned to deliver bad news. "They're going to die," he says, "it's a fact."

At 5:03 P.M., he inspects a ragged blotch of color on a radar screen. "We've got some semi-ugly stuff coming up very rapidly," he notes with concern. The Texas storm moves closer, narrowing the distance to the southern Oklahoma border. England calls it a "rascal" with a strange kind of affection mingled with respect. It sounds corny, but weathermen bond with these things. The mightiest of these destroyers, after all, live for four to six hours and develop in stages. Early on a storm is like an unformed child, he muses, to grow good or bad depending on its environment. Suspense attends its maturation. Will it or won't it? When a tornado confirms the worst, the excitement levels off in the weather center. The storm has fulfilled its terrible potential; now the public must be warned.

The semi-ugly stuff churns on. We're in a "holding pattern," patiently waiting for the spiky blob on the screen to declare its character. Gary England, a natural storyteller who rarely gets to display these talents on the time-conscious news program, has no problem killing time in a holding pattern. He leans forward, smiles big, and the Okie drawl starts to thicken as he describes how a boy from the little town of Seiling got to be a big-time TV weatherman. Pronounced "ceiling," it's the same place where, on the outskirts of town, saloon-smasher Carry Nation of Prohibition days once lived. Up there in ranch and wheat country, young Gary thought he was going to be a pig farmer. Then he stumbled onto a better profession.

"There used to be a guy on television, Harry Volkman. Sundays he had a 15-minute weather show. We didn't have a television, we lived out in the country. I was in seventh grade, and my daddy took me into town every Sunday to grandma's house to see Harry do the weather. And I just fell in love with it. I didn't even know what it was. One Sunday I said, 'Daddy, I want to be one of those.' He said, 'Well, what is he?' And I said, 'I don't know, but I want to be one.'"

Unfortunately, he wasn't much of a scholar. As a teenager he played halfback on the football team and class clown in the schoolhouse. Unimpressed teachers labeled him bright, but lazy. A belated diagnosis of dyslexia has since explained why he froze up during tests and had to reread textbooks again and again as words jumbled and disappeared. Gary struggled through high school, then did a stint in the Navy weather service. A real sailor's life, he found out to his chagrin, differed a great deal from the dashing cinematic portrayals he was familiar with.

Soon he was back in Oklahoma, attending a state college and working toward winning a degree in meteorology and the affections of a pert and peppy red-haired cheerleader. How they met could have been scripted by a dime-store novelist. During a festive prehomecoming weekend, as Gary was out strolling with a date, Mary Carlisle happened to step from between two parked cars, right into his path. Immediately smitten, he stepped forward and kissed her. On the lips. Twice. His date punched him in the face.

Mary and Gary got married, naturally. And if he ever doubted that his feckless, footloose days were over, Gary was convinced when baby Molly arrived. He took a steady job with a New Orleans firm doing forecasts for the offshore petroleum industry, working for a tough, exacting boss, a man who taught him the skills of discipline and organization he had always lacked. Still, in his heart he longed to be a broadcaster like his idol Harry Volkman.

In 1971 he got a break, of sorts. He had quit the New Orleans job to return to Oklahoma, and a small radio station in the capital hired him to report the weather. His entree into the world of broadcasting couldn't have been any less glamorous. Every day he climbed a set of pull-down stairs in an ordinary garage to reach his attic office, where he hunched over a radar scavenged from an airplane. With its limited range, it could hardly see beyond the city limits. Even worse, he wasn't the glib broadcast personality he had imagined himself to be. He was boring, really boring.

"The program director said, 'Gary, you're never going to make it unless you learn to laugh and have fun.' I was just scared to death. He taught me to laugh on the air and I got a little better. Finally he said, 'I don't think you're ever going to make it. You need more help.'"

"I had a little lizard I had caught at Canton Lake. We nicknamed it a Thunder Lizard. We just basically created this eight-hundred-and-five-pound Thunder Lizard on the radio. On radio you can work people's minds. I'd have that thing out every morning, it'd be on Interstate 35, chasing Coors Beer trucks. People at the gas station would call in and claim they saw it. It was really wild, crazy stuff. One day the boss at the radio station said, 'Not enough people know who you are.' I thought, 'What can I do?' I picked a beautiful, sunny summer afternoon, about 95 degrees, not a cloud in the sky. And about 5 P.M. I ran the tornado warning beeps. The next day people were saying, 'You have to listen to that fool over on that radio station.'"

His antics won admirers in high places, in the upper ranks of management at KWTV. The station hired him in 1972. He brought along the lizard, of course.

"People wanted to see it. We promoted it some, ran a contest, got about three thousand entries, most of them from people 21 or older. Oils, watercolors, sculptures made out of metal. It was interesting. No one had any idea what this thing looked like. Some were really scary. About that time I decided we'd have some fun, so I took a cameraman outside, a cold October day, wind blowing. This guy was a great actor. He had on cowboy boots, Levis, and this big ol' sheepskin coat, and he had long blond curls and a hat on, and a big ol' beer potbelly. I interviewed him. 'Sir, I understand you saw something.' 'Yes, sir.' He's making this up. He said, 'I's driving my car home at 2 A.M. and something ran across the road. It was so big I've been driving my pickup ever since.' 'How big do you think it was?' 'Oh, about eight hundred and five pounds.' Finally I said, 'What was it?' And he just kind of kicked gravel, then he looked right at the camera: 'I believe it was an eight-hundred-and-five-pound Thunder Lizard.' And I ran that on the six o'clock news. It jammed the phone lines. The UFO people called. And people went to work the next day, saying that on Channel 9, this guy's got this huge lizard that came in on a spaceship. The key is they talked. And they started tuning in."

And Gary England turned into a sensation. Eventually he retired the half-ton Thunder Lizard for an animal that exists independently of the imagination, a black Vietnamese potbellied pig nicknamed Spike the Wonder Pig. He began touring a tornado video show that each spring arrives in small towns with all the fanfare of a Lollapalooza concert. Tall speakers mightily reverberate gym floors as twisters smash and swing across a giant screen. Afterwards, England signs autographs for a mobbing, adoring crowd. Along with all this, he has managed to pen a couple of slim books, *Oklahoma Weather* and *Those Terrible Twisters*.

Why anyone should care about the rise of Gary England is, simply, he's a uniquely Oklahoma creation, the local weatherman as celebrity and hero. Anywhere else his evening reports would be just a footnote to the news of the day. His would be a forgettable face, interchangeable with any of his genial and well-coifed competitors. Here, Gary England rode severe weather and the threat of the terrible twister to a monstrous fame. In one KWTV survey more people knew his name than that of the state governor.

In the middle of storm country, England and his fellow weathercasters are something more than popular, treasured messengers, however. They deliver the severe weather gospel for many Oklahomans, who will not be sucked up in a tornado or even personally glimpse one. They define what ordinary people know about tornadoes and what they need to know. What the TV meteorologists report about the danger, what they advise about taking shelter, this all becomes the common truth on the street.

It's almost time for a weather update, and England tilts back his head and blinks down eye drops. A tornado watch has been issued, but the only line of storms in Oklahoma is almost humdrum for this time of year. By telephone Dalrymple arranges for live video when the line "comes walking across the city."

A technician wheels a tall camera apparatus to the open door of the forecast center. A floodlight flashes on, and the room seems like a darkened theater stage thrown into harsh brightness. The color drains from England's already pale face. He leans forward and concentrates, no script in hand.

"All right, let's check out the tornado watch," he begins briskly, and rattles through the list of Oklahoma counties under tornado watch number 289, issued at 3:30 P.M. A readout from his prized Doppler 9000 then fills the viewing screen. He smoothly translates what it sees: storms approaching the metro area at 30 miles an hour, to arrive within the hour. They're not severe, he reassures. "We'll have more weather as required," he wraps up.

He unclips a small tie microphone. The weather shift now belongs solely to Mitchell. The storms are weakly folding up. England tears hungrily into a bagel. When a KWTV storm crew at Altus calls for instructions, without hesitation he replies, "Bring 'em home." Mitchell thinks the watch may be canceled because, as the sun sets, the atmosphere loses its destabilizing heat source. The storms are stumpy anyway. Their tops reach only 30,000 feet.

Another spring day draws to a close. England disappears, running to catch an outdoor wedding reception in progress, more worried about a wayward shower than a twister. Mitchell prepares for another lonely Saturday night at the helm. He is one in what will become a long line of weather messengers at KWTV and KFOR and others. Each spring, viewers know that their guardians are looking out for them by an icon hanging in the corner of the television screen, color coded for a variety of watches and warnings, or a bulletin crawling in ticker-tape fashion across the bottom of the screen. Or a weatherman breaks unexpectedly into a favorite prime-time program. But despite the complaints that you hear—that this weather coverage business is really out of hand, that a bulletin is creeping across somebody's attempt to videotape *Rambo*, or that nobody wants to hear about a little storm in some two-bit town—despite all that, Oklahomans have a superb warning system. And you know, deep down, no one living in the shadow of the tornado really wants to lose that.

Storm Chasers

9

Chasing the Wind

Behind the making of the tornado warning system in Oklahoma is another story, one unrelated to Gary England or frenzied television ratings wars. Its heroes are research meteorologists who toiled for years in near obscurity, approaching the most violent thunderstorms they could find, then patiently observing and waiting. They sought a difficult and elusive answer to a simple question: How and why does a tornado spin up? And, in trying to puzzle this out, they turned into storm chasers.

They believed they had to, despite the personal risk. Hoping for a twister to pass conveniently over a fixed weather station was almost like sitting outdoors in the rain and watching for lightning to hit a particular tree in a forest. Their luck was dismal. Finally it occurred to them to improve their odds by carrying their notepads and sensitive instruments right to the source. As one later remarked, if the mountain won't come to you, you go to the mountain.

Of course, upon closer inspection that sentiment is more noble than practical. The tornado is certainly not a solid, immobile object, to be scaled at one's leisure. On the contrary, a funnel slithers with unpredictable strength out of a huge, chaotic cloud. It strikes fast and dissipates, or makes a sudden turn. Hunting down tornadoes thus meant running two quite different risks, of never seeing one at all, or worse, of accidentally being swallowed.

Fortunately the former proved to be a greater problem for pioneer storm chaser Neil Ward, a native of Lexington, in central

Oklahoma. He was a rather short, shy man with a high forehead and clear, frank brown eyes. His Oklahoma pedigree was indisputable. He had been educated in a one-room schoolhouse and had a grandfather who staked a claim in the 1889 land run. Nearing his fortieth birthday, Ward began to investigate another distinctive Sooner State event, the tornado. At first he didn't go out looking for them, but rather observed small, captive specimens in his garage.

The time was the early 1950s. After a respectable, if unspectacular 13-year career with the United States Weather Bureau, Ward had decided to take on a specialty. He was tired of traveling across the country in a van, calibrating instruments at weather service offices. Since he loved to tinker with pulleys and engines and machines, he built a low-budget tornado model. To do so, he had to manipulate air to create a flow resembling that of the most intense storm for its size known to man. His solution was elegant in its simplicity.

First, a nonmeteorologist has to understand that the vortex (the broad class of fluids rotating around an axis, to which the tornado belongs) is far from being an unusual occurrence. In fact, a vortex seeker need look no farther than a whirlpool created over the drain of an emptying bathtub. Ward knew that, to accomplish his objective, he needed only to simulate the simplest atmospheric conditions.

He cut out two plywood circles, each about the size of a wagon wheel. He mounted one of them eight inches above the other. The lower disk crudely represented the ground, and the upper the sky. Between them, his tornado would form. In the "ground" disk he drilled a hole for a smoke tube. In a normal tornado, condensing water vapor renders the funnel visible. In a model on the small scale of his, Ward knew he would need some help in the form of a smoke tracer to show the presence of the spinning air.

That settled, he turned his attention to the upper plywood circle, the "sky" disk. It functioned similarly to a blocking inversion in the atmosphere. No air could pass up through the plywood—unless he let it. He cut out an opening to parallel what happens in the atmosphere when a powerful updraft punches through a hole in the inversion. In this updraft a tornado forms.

To allow variable sizes for his miniature updrafts, he fitted an adjustable camera-like iris in the opening.

What would make the air rise through that hole? He solved this by installing an electrical-powered chimney overhead. It heated air, which then rose naturally. His tornado chamber was ready. Almost. Ward realized he lacked a crucial element. A chimney supplied rising hot air, to which he needed to impart the critical property of *spin* in order to make a tornado.

That, too, was not an insurmountable obstacle. The solution didn't endear him to his teenage son Bob, pieces of whose train set migrated from the house to the garage. Ward selected curved track sections and snapped them together. He created a raised course that curled around the perimeter of the upper plywood disk. He placed on the tracks the trucks from several model railroad cars, and they looped around and around, like some kind of an elevated train going nowhere forever in an M.C. Escher drawing.

What mattered most was the cargo the trucks bore, a flat metal donut with sheet metal fins hanging down. Any air streaming into the space between the "ground" and "sky" plywood disks first had to pass through the revolving fins. In doing so, it acquired a little spin. That spin tightened and quickened as the air converged on the center. Then the rotating air rose through the updraft hole.

His model worked. When he puffed smoke in through the tube, lovely shapes no taller than his forearm began to twist hypnotically. They looked like undulating snakes, swaying filaments, and even a vertical sine curve. He controlled their behavior by adjusting the metal iris opening from three to sixteen inches in diameter and by varying the rotation speed of the fins. A wide hole and fast rotation produced a large-mouthed, turbulent funnel. A small hole and slow rotation spawned a slender, twisting stalk. Ward hated cigarette smoke, but in the name of science, he would choke through a couple of packs during each session to create his whirls.

The model transformed him into a local celebrity. The press lavished wondrous praise on him with newspaper articles and headlines like "Don't Fret! It's Tame . . . Sooner Hatches a Real Tornado." It was a big career break for Ward, a skilled, avid

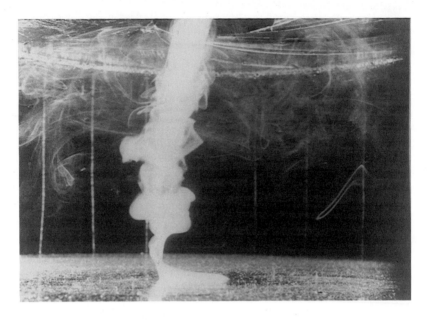

Neil Ward's early tornado model.   *History of Science Collections,*
University of Oklahoma Libraries

forecaster who nevertheless felt handicapped by not having an
undergraduate degree. He had never finished course work for a
bachelor's in mechanical engineering and, to worsen matters,
found himself easing into middle age without any prestigious
accomplishments to his name. Now he could proudly point to his
model. Much impressed, the Weather Bureau awarded him
scholarships to take graduate-level courses in fluid mechanics, so
he could understand the physical laws governing complex air
flows.

His two children Bob and Jean, knowing nothing about the
finer points of atmospheric physics, just enjoyed hanging around
the garage while their father worked. They watched him tinker
as fans whirred and motors hummed. Ward flipped on switches
for light bulbs carefully placed above and to the side of the chamber, behind which the garage wall was painted black to contrast
with the smoky-white tornadoes. He crouched down and shot

black-and-white slides and 16-millimeter movies of their gyrations.

Anytime he wasn't preoccupied with his miniature twisters, Ward indulged more ordinary tastes and attended to domestic chores. He would take off a day from work to run a few cattle to market, or spend a morning driving the tractor, towing a disk harrow that broke up garden soil to prepare for a fresh crop of potatoes, corn, okra, tomatoes, radishes, and onions. He liked to cook and read history books with a passion, especially stories about the Old West and Billy the Kid. On family vacations, he always insisted on taking long detours just to read historical markers.

Those vacations were also memorable for sightings of dust devils—whirling, unstable columns of air that form on hot days over desertlike terrain in the southwest. Ward would stop on the side of the road, then photograph or try to run into the whirl. On one occasion, he spotted an abnormally large dust demon some 30 feet wide. Excited, he pulled over the car and jumped out. He chased it on foot, but to no avail. From her seat his wife Obera watched it close in, swallow the car, then cross the road with her husband close behind.

Such unusual behavior may have seemed frivolous to the average person, but not to Ward's employer. Hoping that circulation patterns in dust whirls could offer clues to what causes severe storms, the Weather Bureau supported him in field studies. Ward and a partner requisitioned a special Army rifle, with which they fired colored smoke grenades into the top of the spinning columns to better resolve the interweaving wind flows. While roaming southern New Mexico and west Texas in the summer of 1960, they scored a major triumph. They found a dust devil so large it contained multiple vortices.

All the same, a dust devil, no matter how impressive, doesn't begin to measure up to a tornado. It doesn't arise from the same kind of instabilities and doesn't hang from a thunderstorm. It's a fairly harmless hot-weather phenomenon, a useful curiosity to a point. If Ward wanted a tornado, he needed to go out and find one. He finally got a chance by transferring in 1960 to the Norman, Oklahoma, branch of the weather service's newly created National Severe Storms Project. As a radar meteorologist, he was charged with gathering data and doing research.

Radar had been nothing short of revolutionary in its impact on storm warnings. In the field of meteorology, it was one of the two enduring legacies of World War II (the other, the computer, revolutionized the art of forecasting by being able to run realistic numerical models of the complex atmosphere). The same technology that identified approaching hostile planes also picked out growing storms on the march. In the late 1950s the Weather Bureau began setting up a national network of WSR-57s, or weather surveillance radars. The WSR-57 took a kind of X-ray of a severe thunderstorm, but in the resulting amoeba-shaped image, meteorologists had to verify where a tornado might be lurking. They needed ground-truth information. In other words, what did someone standing outside, looking at the storm, actually see?

Neil Ward was only too happy to assist in this effort. On May 4, 1961, when a north-south line of storms flared up west of Oklahoma City, a highway patrol car raced toward the roughest-looking cell. Ward was riding in the front seat. From time to time the radio crackled to life with directions and observations from a radar operator back in Oklahoma City. Then the operator noticed a suspicious hook-shaped area of precipitation developing on his screen. Ward looked out, and northwest of Geary, ragged clouds were struggling down from a low cloud base. The funnel touched down, then lifted and dangled as it crossed the highway, only one-half mile away. They took off in pursuit, and several more twisters formed before darkness overtook them. Ward had just become the first trained meteorologist to track down a tornado in a ground vehicle.

This easy success whetted his thirst, and Ward continued his investigations. He took as a partner Charles Clark, a former Air Force meteorologist who had once hidden in a ditch in Georgia as a tornado flipped fire trucks and tore up buildings on the base around him. The two men gamely set out in Ward's little Ford Anglia. Clark read the maps and took the photographs, Ward watched the sky and drove.

Reaching their objective quickly turned into an exercise in exasperation. The thunderclouds hurtled along at speeds up to 50 miles an hour on straight-line paths that all too seldom coincided with the doglegs and twists of the highway below. To catch up, Ward boldly steered the Anglia down unmarked dirt roads, and they often discovered too late what a trap the storm had laid out there, acres of fresh mud waiting like quicksand. Sometimes their shortcut fizzled out at a dead end.

When the storm trackers were given a specially equipped government van, their spirits were lifted, but then they discovered its limitations. A powerful two-way radio was supposed to connect them to the control room in Norman. This link was vital for receiving directions on where to go and for correlating observations out in open country with radar screen pictures. No more did they have to fumble coins out of their pockets at roadside pay phones. But right from the beginning the system proved almost comically inadequate. Via the ionosphere they were able to contact New Orleans, five hundred miles away, but often not Norman, eighteen miles away, because of static from lightning. Whenever a clear channel was secured, the energy of their talking voices flooded the radarscope and garbled critical data that had to be preserved. Just when it seemed things couldn't get any worse, they forgot to lower the 25-foot radio antenna and an overpass clipped it off.

Even a perfect connection wouldn't have changed the fact that the storm chasers were coming up empty handed. One day they came close to their goal, after a brief halt occasioned by a burst of large hail. They photographed some specimens, wrapped them in a horse blanket, then hurried off on their way. Topping a hill, they saw a man standing in bafflement in the road. Ward cranked down the window.

"Did a storm just pass through here?" he asked.

"A tornado."

"A tornado?"

"There's not a window in my house," the man replied. The meteorologists looked. Curtains flapped freely through broken glass. His driveway, over which he had recently spread a coat of gravel, was as bare as if it had been painstakingly swept with a broom.

Ward and Clark moved on, creeping over electrical lines thrown over the roadway and maneuvering past prostrated trees and telephone poles. At the next intersection people were climbing out of a storm cellar next to a smooth concrete pad. Low on gas, Ward pulled up and asked where the nearest filling station was. "It was right here," answered a woman.

The difficulty he was having only served to further convince Ward that he couldn't confine his excursions to business hours. Success largely depended on variables beyond his control, like plain old luck and good timing. When a tornado was reported near his Lexington home, he quickly accepted a neighbor's offer to drive him to the site. Minutes later they located it. Ward balanced in the bed of the moving pickup with a camera as the increasingly nervous neighbor cast worried glances over his shoulder. The meteorologist leaned down and yelled through the open window, "When you get to the next section line, make a left! I want to get a picture of it coming at us!" The driver was relieved to find no left at the next section line. He never volunteered to take out Ward again.

But a development in 1964 made it appear likely that Ward would soon have plenty of storm-chasing companions. His employer, the National Severe Storms Project, changed its name—to the National Severe Storms Laboratory—and more significantly, its location. It had been headquartered in Kansas City, where the heavy air traffic and the dense population hindered its usefulness for field investigations. Norman, its new home, was relatively uncluttered and open, with a fledgling meteorology department at the University of Oklahoma to tap into for talent. As for Ward, he was delighted to have the major severe storms research facility in the country only a half-hour drive from his house.

If it seemed too good to be true, it was. His pet loves were not embraced by Ed Kessler, the first director of NSSL. Kessler resisted Ward's suggestion that storm chasing become an integral part of its research. To Kessler's way of thinking, NSSL had greater priorities, such as the development of a promising new kind of radar known as Doppler and the study of lightning, which had caused recent turbojet accidents. He nixed as well the senior scientist's idea to take on as a project the construction of a better tornado model.

Ward insisted stubbornly that, one way or another, he was going to build it.

"Fine, Neil," Kessler said. "I commend you for that. I could be wrong. But I have to do my job as I see it."

And so a new, much larger tornado model appeared in the Lexington garage. It was five feet tall and eight feet wide, with a brand new feature, a honeycomb screen. This was an ingenious solution to the problem of how, at some height, to get the tornado to stop turning. In the atmosphere storm winds diverge at the upper edge of the troposphere, a good eight miles above the earth, and cause the rotating column to slow, much like an ice skater coming out of a spin. Yet laboratory models had failed to reflect that. They neglected to divorce the tiny tornado from a spinning fan that pulled air through the model. Ward's honeycomb tubes positioned below the fan, on the other hand, perfectly disrupted the air passing through them. They removed the twist from the top of the twister.

This striking feature opened up a whole new world to Ward. He could now imitate, with decent verisimilitude, the large multiple-vortex tornadoes that occur in nature. And he could show how a single-vortex tornado changes into a multiple-vortex. It was a fascinating transition to behold. First, the slim tornado broadened, air flowing down at its core. Visually, it resembled a steady snake swallowing a vibrating egg. The egg was the bulge, or in scientific terms the breakdown, pushing toward the ground with increasing swirl. With it came a more unsteady flow, until finally a thin snake had transformed into a turbulent ball of vapor.

Learning of the model's sophistication, Kessler relented. He allowed Ward to work on it in a laboratory on the University of Oklahoma campus. There, the tornado chamber attracted the attention of curious meteorology students like Chuck Doswell. Ward patiently explained how it worked to Doswell, a tall, rangy, bright iconoclast with long hair and a full Fu Manchu mustache. Doswell had resumed his doctoral studies after an involuntary tour of duty in Vietnam he liked to refer sardonically to as his "enforced sabbatical."

"I think the thing that stands out most in my mind was when Ward told me that the smoke he was using was some kind of really toxic substance. I remember thinking about this. He had this big fan that sucked it all up, then blew it out the window.

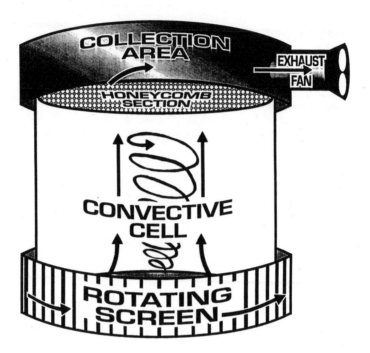

Diagram of Neil Ward's tornado model with honeycomb innovation.
Mark Loftis

Here was this toxic stuff, titanium something, it was really
nasty. I remember thinking not to go by there at night when he
was running his experiments."

That toxic substance was a corrosive compound, titanium
tetrachloride, that ate holes in all kinds of metal in the lab. It
was a colorless liquid that fumed when exposed to moist air and
acted for Ward as a better tracer than cigarette smoke. On the
lab floor, he would start a heavy titanium tetrachloride fog that
slowly spread out at ground level before being sucked up into the
vortex. He preferred running his experiments at night when the
atmosphere was more settled and the building empty, so shut-
ting doors did not cause small pressure waves that his sensitive
instruments would register.

In idle moments, Ward not only willingly shared his knowledge with students who came to regard him as a mentor, but with letter writers to NSSL. Some were children who asked simple but earnest questions; others rambled on about ill-conceived schemes to harness a tornado's winds or inquired about how to make one themselves, as if they needed only a backyard bonfire and an extra-large bellows. But one of the most embarrassing letters Ward had to handle, he wrote himself.

It was prompted by a casual discussion, the sort that the meteorologists might have while walking back from lunch, matching wits by guessing how far away a distant thunderstorm was, then consulting the radar at the office to determine the winner. This time, the brightest storm researchers in the country wanted to know if the famed *Wizard of Oz* tornado was real. If so, when was the film shot and by whom? Kessler assigned Ward to find out, and his letter to MGM came back with a note scrawled across the bottom of the page. "A nice compliment!" wrote Buddy Gillespie, the mastermind behind the fake. Gillespie's response was short, but had he wanted to, he could have filled a page or two about the frustration of creating a tornado from scratch in 1938.

This particular story was a testament to the power of creative genius in a low-tech special-effects era. The first attempt on an MGM studio stage was an $8,000, four-story rubber cone shaped like a wind sock. That stiff twister flunked the key litmus test: it wouldn't twist. Gillespie switched materials, substituting the fabric muslin in place of rubber. The muslin cone twisted too freely, so it was interlaced with music wire for rigidity. The top of the giant wind sock was then attached to a movable gantry so as to allow it to move independently of the bottom, which disappeared through a slot on the stage floor. The tornado could sway, and did, as it menaced a miniature set. Dorothy's Kansas house was less than three feet high, and corn stalks no taller than a finger. Film of the tornado was shot and specially processed for use as a background. That enabled a real, live Judy Garland to flee a tornado that was just a clever fake projected onto a screen behind her.

That was Hollywood fantasy at its best. Neil Ward and his associates had no use for glamor and gadgetry. They engaged in

A rather unusual-looking multiple-vortex tornado created by Neil Ward in his later model. *History of Science Collections, University of Oklahoma Libraries*

science, in the methodical appraisal of data and the careful evaluation of theories. Then in the spring of 1971, a proposal arrived at the National Severe Storms Laboratory that could have been the grist for a Hollywood script not as fanciful, but every bit as exciting as *The Wizard of Oz*. Bruce Morgan, an assistant professor in the engineering department at the University of Notre Dame, wanted to enlist NSSL's help in catching a tornado—and driving straight into it.

Ed Kessler called into his office Joe Golden, a young research meteorologist finishing up a doctoral dissertation on waterspouts.

"Joe, I've gotten a lot of harebrained proposals," Kessler said, handing over the 47-page, neatly typed, illustrated proposal. "This may be another one."

Golden flipped through it with mounting disbelief. Morgan

wanted to drive into a tornado in a surplus M59, a 21-ton military personnel carrier with plate armor up to five-eighths of an
inch thick. "The M59 is ideally suited to this task," Morgan
pitched. "Heavily armored, it is designed to carry twelve soldiers
directly into enemy fire." It moved 30 miles an hour, was outfit-
ted with multiple periscopes, and climbed steep grades. There
was even a photograph of it afloat.

The strategy was this: A flatbed trailer truck carrying the
tanklike vehicle would close to within sighting distance of the
tornado. The M59 would then lumber off a rear ramp and take
off. Its operators would have a two-way radio for communications and a camera for filming their approach. The retrofitted
military vehicle promised to be a dramatic sight moving over the
prairie, sporting two outsized propeller anemometers, a blinking
exterior strobe light, and a thick, towering boom packed with
weather instruments.

A good deal of skepticism met the Morgan proposal when it
was circulated for review among select scientists, including Neil
Ward and Bob Davies-Jones, a recent hire. Davies-Jones was a
lean, sharp-eyed Englishman with a dry wit and a keen, theoret-
ical mind. He contested Morgan's rosy predictions of success,
based on computer simulations. What if the funnel skipped over
the M59 at the last second? Or what about the problem of acces-
sibility? A ground approach could be thwarted upon encounter-
ing a farmer's fence or a patch of woods. Furthermore, section
roads that Morgan relied on were known to be primitive and
treacherous, and some bridges over creeks would probably collapse under a loaded trailer truck's weight.

Another reviewer pondered what might be in store for the
intrepid team members in a 21-ton vehicle if they did manage to
reach their target. Strong tornadoes play notoriously rough. A
25-ton ferryboat was thrown by one in Venice, Italy. A Lubbock,
Texas, tornado hurled a 16-ton fertilizer tank seven hundred
yards through the air. Even more disturbing, an armored personnel carrier had been lifted before, in a 1949 twister right in
Norman. If the M59 flipped or rolled, it would be more vulnerable to flying debris. The plate armor on the top was only three-
eighths of an inch thick.

Beyond the threat of personal harm to participants, the

whole idea threatened to be an utter public relations disaster, an M59 charging across private land and chewing through wheat fields like an elephant running amok. For his part, NSSL director Kessler revived an old objection about storm chasing, whether Neil Ward did it in a small car or Bruce Morgan ordered up a fleet of Army tanks. He feared an angry public would protest, "You guys are a bunch of storm jocks. What the hell are you doing wasting the taxpayers' money?"

What did impress Kessler, at least somewhat, were Morgan's computer trials. The Notre Dame engineer calculated that vehicles, pursuing at reasonable speeds, stood a 90 percent chance of intercepting randomly generated Oklahoma tornadoes in a given year. Even after revising downward this figure, Kessler thought storm chasing looked feasible. He consented to try it, but drew up a new set of rules. No M59. No $90,000 budget, which was what Morgan originally requested. And the chasers had to confine their range to within Oklahoma.

The approved project hardly resembled the one Morgan proposed. He received three thousand dollars for a one-year trial, and a Dodge Sportsman Wagon with power steering and mud-grip tires. The driver was to stop, naturally, well before reaching the tornado. Joe Golden reluctantly took the role of "cognizant scientist" in charge of overseeing the progress of the project and reporting back to Kessler. He hoped that being associated with the underfunded, dubious undertaking wasn't going to damage his future career. He did have to admit that their chances of measuring a tornado in the field were better than waiting for one to happen to pass over one of the unmanned weather stations clustered around Oklahoma City.

Finally Neil Ward's judgment was being vindicated. Organized storm chasing was about to begin, and his latest tornado model was winning acclaim. He should have enjoyed the year 1972, but ever since he was a teenager, his heart had been behaving strangely, skipping beats and palpitating oddly. As he aged, heart disease sapped his strength. In the fall of 1971 he had to undergo open heart surgery. After the operation Ward, groggy and hurting in his hospital bed, told his daughter Jean it hadn't been worth it. He returned to work, but died in the spring of 1972 at the age of 57.

Too long during his lifetime had he tried to shed a nagging feeling of inferiority. He was an anomaly—a researcher at a prestigious institution without even a college diploma—and he knew it. His coworkers had bouquets of graduate degrees. Yet in the end Ward proved that his mind was as fertile and discerning as any of theirs, and even if he stumbled with a formula or two, he possessed sharp observational skills and an ability to isolate what really mattered in solving a problem. His body was laid to rest April 14, the first day of NSSL's Tornado Intercept Project. That afternoon, a dryline threatened to help fire up thunderstorms. It moved east over a freshly heaped grave in the Lexington cemetery, then quietly retreated. Later, under the cloak of night, storms broke out.

In the days to come, Ward was missed not only for his genial, unassuming manner, but for his storm-chasing expertise. The first intercept crews did a fair bit of blundering about. They were trying to reconcile their textbook training with the fantastic and varied cloud shapes they were seeing. Real weather, they learned soon enough, didn't fit into easy categories. In a perfect world the tornado would dangle neatly from a rainfree base and be visible many miles away. More often than not, what they got were wet, messy storms that shrouded everything in veils of rain. University of Oklahoma student Chuck Doswell, riding in the Dodge Sportsman, peered through the windows more than once in curious puzzlement.

"You had this terrible sense that something really neat was happening somewhere else and you just didn't know it because you didn't see it. None of us had a clear idea of the relationship of the tornado to the storm. We didn't know beans. We were kind of wildly guessing what to do, where to look. We fortunately survived and didn't do anything grossly stupid."

The storm chasers were dedicated, if somewhat odd and overexuberant. They brought their own still cameras, with the understanding that any good photographs would be shared. Most of their meager funds went for fuel. An NSSL administrator, Dorothy Alexander, served as their driver with the reflexive obedience of a good soldier. If Golden pointed to a low, ugly lip of cloud jutting out of the storm and said, "Dorothy, I really want to get to that," she drove straight in without a squawk of protest.

She was steady and unflappable, and sometimes seemed ready
to turn around and snap, "Calm down!" to her excitable passen-
gers.

Meanwhile, senior meteorologists looked on with disdain as
the project fired the imaginations of their younger colleagues,
who found an ample supply of gung-ho OU meteorology students
to accompany them. Golden, no longer a skeptic, was dragging
researchers from their work stations to watch thunderstorm
films he procured. The older scientists steadfastly resisted the
overtures. In their eyes, hunting for a tornado was an exercise in
futility and soft science to boot—a glorified photography field
trip. They respected experiments that generated hard quantitative data that fit into equations, that proved or disproved hy-
potheses.

They remained unconvinced even after an early, impressive
success. On April 30, the roving NSSL crew, in a harrowing
maneuver, plunged through a hail-filled storm core. On the other
side was luckily clear air and, to the west, a tornado forming
from a rotating, bell-shaped cumulonimbus. Just before sunset
the funnel spiked down against a softly luminous sky. Another
successful intercept followed a month later, and funding came
for an additional year of trials.

Golden seized the opportunity to attempt to collect better
data. He wisely contacted NASA, the government agency most
favored with useful new technology, and arranged to borrow at
little cost a $30,000 movie camera used on the Apollo space
mission. Magazines for the camera, loaded with high-resolution
film, were designed to snap rapidly in and out. The storm hunters had the equipment, the experience, and more confidence.
Now they needed the right tornado to silence the critics.

On May 24, 1973, it arrived on an unusual violent weather
day for Oklahoma. The jet streams were all wrong, far to the
north in Nebraska and deep in southern Texas. But a small area
of low pressure crossing the state set off a long chain of strong
thunderstorms. At two o'clock, the NSSL intercept crew sped off
from their base with a *Popular Science* writer in the back seat.
They went west, then their radio contact at NSSL spotted an
isolated storm cell vigorously shooting up not far behind them.

"Notch back and south," Golden ordered the driver. "Let's
go!"

They circled around the storm, then raced north toward Union City. NSSL radar was seeing winds whipsawing back and forth in the midlevels of the updraft. South of Union City, they piled out of the vehicle. "It's down!" someone shouted. Two and a half miles away, a sinuous white hose moved with eerie smoothness over the ground. There was a puff, then it darkened with black bits that looked like soil clumps, but were actually remnants of a farmhouse it had just obliterated.

Farther up Highway 81, in a Ford Mustang, a tense drama was being played out at that same moment. Earlier, it had been more like a comedy of errors when the carload of OU students passed right by a mushrooming cumulus near Union City to catch a more robust storm in progress to the north. Upon realizing their tactical mistake, they doubled back. On the way they stopped briefly to photograph a pair of harmless vortices hanging from the anvil, twisted in the shape of sausages extruding a string of cloud. On resuming their approach, they saw that only one map route led to Union City. It ran directly south, through the violent storm core. "Punching the core" has always been as dangerous as it sounds, a vulnerable and blind step into the unknown. They already knew this monster had teeth: a pronounced wall cloud was visible. Still, they weren't about to miss the show, and so the Mustang and its uneasy occupants vanished in dense draperies of rain.

One passenger kept silent, though he was absolutely terrified. Fort Worth native Al Moller knew what an enormous risk they were taking. A year before, on April 19, 1972, the lure was a tantalizing radar echo on the other side of a core. "A persistent hook," reported their excited radar man by radio, "It looks pretty nasty." With that incitement, five college-age kids jammed in a small foreign sedan decided to crash through the shield of precipitation for a closer look.

Matters quickly degraded from bad to worse. Visibility dropped to zero, and Moller held his rear door ajar to help direct the driver onto the shoulder of the highway. There they planned to wait. No sooner had he rolled up his window than a startled voice blurted, "Here it comes!" Over a tree line, flicking off the crowns as it came, rushed a spinning, dirt-flecked cloud. Doors sprang open and everyone scrambled out, mindless of rain and hail still falling, to lay flat in a water-filled ditch. Everyone but Moller. In a panic, he couldn't undo his seat belt. After some hopeless fumbling, he lowered his head onto his lap. The first explosive blast of wind topped one hundred miles an hour and almost rolled the car. He looked up. A billboard snapped loose, then sailed out of sight. Large trees leaped up like ballet dancers. Chilly, wet gusts through an open door threw notebook papers into a swirl around his head. Then the car shuddered in a 70-mile-an-hour wind that descended from out of nowhere from the northwest.

A mesocyclone had lifted overhead. What hit them was probably an associated downburst, rain-filled air in the thunderstorm that evaporates and plummets toward the ground, then spreads outward. The shaken students drew a few ragged breaths and composed themselves. Minutes later they were some miles away, back to the pursuit, staring up at a wide, rotating updraft. Two low clouds flew together, corkscrewing like a helix. "That's going to tornado," Moller said. "Let's get it." He turned around. One of his companions was throwing up. Everyone had had enough. On their return they discovered a tornado had demolished a farmhouse. Its walls and roof sections, they realized, were in that bloated debris cloud passing over the tree line. Moller was the only one of the five ever to chase storms again.

That incident scared him, in a deep way. Near Union City, his heart was racing as hail cracked on the windshield. He knew the tornado would be waiting, like a camouflaged spider staking out a trap. As soon as they cleared the murkiness, he saw it right in front of them, an incredibly tall white tube hanging in the misty air. But it was leaving Union City, tracking southeastward. Its deceptively serene beauty contrasted with rows of houses in the foreground flattened like trampled cardboard boxes.

It was while Moller photographed the receding white column and breathed in the sharp odor of ammonia spewing over wreckage that an irrational fear obsessed him. He became convinced that the tornado was bearing down on Norman, more than 20 miles away, and seeking his neighborhood. He acknowledged the absurdity of this, but at the same time harbored an awful fear that he would return to find nothing there but rubble, his wife among the dead. He later reasoned that his feelings perhaps arose from guilt about his unusual hobby.

The Union City twister killed two people and injured four. It cut a 10-mile path through homes and businesses and flung a large gasoline storage tank half a mile, but its 26 minutes of hell were well documented by the Tornado Intercept Project, which finally earned the respect of skeptical senior NSSL meteorologists. The Union City findings represented a real breakthrough in efforts to understand tornado dynamics. It remains the most famous event in the history of organized storm chasing.

For once, virtually everything had gone right. The intercept team watched the tornado from birth to death and filmed its life cycle, a first. The severe storms laboratory Doppler radar was at a close enough range to provide copious details of the thunderstorm's structure. And the high-resolution film shot on the NASA camera was good enough to apply to it a sophisticated technique called photogrammetry. In this procedure used to calculate wind speed, one measures how far debris travels from one film frame to the next, and figures in the distance to the tornado, and angles to stationary objects in the frame like a barn or telephone pole. Photogrammetry showed the Union City tornado was whirling at more than 175 miles an hour.

Crowning the team's achievements was a *Popular Science* article published in the fall that wove a flattering portrayal of the National Severe Storms Laboratory and its mission through a gripping narrative of the expedition. Ed Kessler discovered that his old concerns were groundless. No angry public materialized to complain that tax dollars were being frittered away. Rather, the meteorologists were perceived as heroes, daring to take risks on the wild frontier of severe weather research. Kessler later reflected that, over the years, the storm-chasing program absorbed 1 percent of NSSL's budget while accounting for 50 percent of its publicity, largely positive.

Through the 1970s the meteorologists continued to roam the interstates and back roads of Oklahoma, looking for trouble in the sky. They observed and filmed a spectacular array of severe thunderstorms and tried to verify what the Doppler radar in Norman was indicating. In 1977, the project was joined by a newcomer to the region and to the University of Oklahoma faculty. Howard Bluestein was schooled at MIT, where he had worked with lasers and holograms and written a master's thesis on predicting cloud motions from satellite photographs. The Boston native looked the part of the storm chaser, with unkempt hair, a swarthy face that tanned easily, and a gently amused expression. But his first outing left him slightly dispirited.

"My two most permanent impressions were one, that I hated to drive long distances. I wasn't used to driving four, five hundred miles in the same day and winding up back at the same place. The other was that my group was restricted to an area covered by the Doppler radar at NSSL. And it seemed like all the good storms were outside of our area."

Bluestein was a little late on the scene, but a quick study. He prolonged his stay at the university beyond one year, and soon began ambitiously designing his own projects within those conducted by NSSL. In his quest for quantitative data, he undertook a bold, unusual experiment. He wanted measurements of the violent tornado core, so he decided to try to get them—by proxy.

The sacrificial lamb was going to be TOTO, an instrumented metal barrel. Toto was the name of Dorothy's cuddly cairn terrier in *The Wizard of Oz*, but in this context meant TOtable Tornado Observatory. Anchored in a sturdy cage, it was designed to survive a direct tornado strike with recordings of air pressure, temperature, and wind velocity.

For three springs in the early 1980s, Bluestein and his crew hurriedly placed TOTO as close to oncoming twisters as they safely could. It took only half a minute to roll the four-hundred-pound device off the back of their pickup truck before they could speed away, out of danger. TOTO waited on more than one Oklahoma roadside to make meteorological history, but with disappointing results.

The experiment never overcame serious flaws in concept and design. Laws of probability militated against TOTO's being hit. Over the course of the mile or so a tornado had to track to reach the device, it might veer, lift, or dissipate. Worse, when TOTO was tested in a laboratory wind tunnel, it tipped over in winds of 110 miles an hour. Even if TOTO escaped being hurled through the air or mutilated by flying debris, chances were good it would end up on its back. It was finally retired and shipped to Washington, D.C., where it sits in the National Oceanic and Atmospheric Administration headquarters as an odd artifact from the early age of storm intercepts.

Bluestein had better luck in the field with a short-wavelength Doppler radar built by the Los Alamos National Laboratory. It was virtually a hundred-pound radar-in-a-suitcase, with sending and receiving dishes the width of large pizza pie pans and a set-up time of three minutes. Being portable, it solved the vexing problem of what to do when tornadoes don't happen to drop near fixed radars. On top of that, it permitted measurements of the very low-level winds, feet above the ground, that play a critical role in tornado formation. A distant radar is unable to do that because straight beams can't follow the curvature of the earth. On April 26, 1991, the Doppler was used to scan the fat trunk of a multiple-vortex tornado that crossed the path of Bluestein's perfectly positioned crew. A spectrum analysis revealed winds of 280 miles an hour, the highest ever measured.

But studying tornadoes was like doing battle with the mythical Hydra, which sprouted two heads for each one lopped off. Researchers were discovering an unending, frustrating tangle of complexities and questions. For instance, these whirls properly fell into more than one class. "Gustnado" described a short-lived (less than a minute), relatively weak tornado along the gust front, the leading edge of the rain-cooled air exiting the base of the storm. Another kind of small tornado, commonly found in eastern Colorado, was dubbed a "landspout" for its similarity in appearance and dynamics to a waterspout.

Meteorologists trained their attention on the deadliest class, that of whirls preceded by ominous, rotating wall clouds that signal the presence of a mesocyclone. And more mysteries bobbed up. Only one-quarter to one-half of all mesocyclones spawn tornadoes. Why those, and why not others? And in the five, ten, or twenty minutes before a tornado spins up, what exactly was happening in the thin layer of air just above the ground to aid this process? And what about the core, the objective for the military vehicle proposal that never got off the drawing board and for hapless TOTO—what was buried in all that sound and fury, and what did it mean?

Answers may be forthcoming. During the springs of 1994

and 1995, the most ambitious storm-chasing project ever was conducted. It sampled from the latest technologies to create an efficient, military-like operation that would have pleasantly surprised Neil Ward with its scope, manpower, and materiel. Its long name was Verification of the Origins of Rotation in Tornadoes Experiment—or, more commonly, VORTEX.

At the first hint of unsettled weather, an armada of up to 20 vans and cars rolled out of the NSSL parking lot in Norman. Occasionally a spooked motorist hastily pulled over to let pass the convoy, which looked as if it was streaming off toward some apocalyptic battle. On many roofs towered a bizarre-looking superstructure of weather instruments. Every six seconds the instruments relayed a full complement of atmospheric readings into the memory chips of onboard laptops.

VORTEX was certainly a serious endeavor, operating under a strict organizational structure and communications protocol. All teams had to obey radio commands from a field coordinator. From his mobile van, he steered them to a broad target area, sometimes hundreds of miles away. On the journey, he tracked each vehicle's position on his customized computer map, which was so detailed that it included foot paths and cemeteries. Satellite positioning technology fixed the location of each armada member with pinpoint accuracy.

Once near its destination, the tightly clustered procession splintered. Teams halted, advanced, and peeled right or left to execute specialized missions. This strategy was the equivalent of flinging a wide net over the giant thunderstorm to capture it for study. Since that was literally impossible, they instead probed it from many perspectives, like a band of latter-day Lilliputians seeking to divine through inexhaustible examination the essence of a strange behemoth in their presence.

Large weather balloons were released into the storm's rushing updraft. Movie crews staked out different angles on the twister for filming; later, wind speeds would be calculated through stereo photogrammetry. By air a plane that once stalked hurricanes scanned the storm with a special radar. On the ground "probe" cars braved vicious wind gusts and damaging hail to trace patterns, like football wide receivers running a play. All the while, their twirling rooftop instruments collected a

VORTEX "probe" car. *Matt Biddle*

wealth of data. The probes crisscrossed boundaries between small warm and cold zones at the surface, places where pre-tornado blobs of air may start spinning.

A successor to TOTO, the turtle, emerged as the latest suicide jockey in the attempt to penetrate a tornado core. Turtles, so named for their pod shape, had tough, lead-lined aluminum shells that protected the tender "meat," the fragile sensors and circuitry inside. They hugged the ground to prevent being easily lifted and thrown, and were painted a bright orange for easy retrieval. With turtles, meteorologists were still gambling, but more wisely. In the path of an advancing whirl they laid down not one, but nine of these low-cost packages, spaced at intervals of several hundred yards.

At the conclusion of VORTEX, researchers had encyclopedic

data sets for a handful of supercells and tornadoes, to form a kind of connect-the-dots picture. How those thousands of dots should be connected to recreate a living, evolving storm will engage scientists for decades to come. In this profusion of numbers they will pan for clues about how a tornado takes shape amidst fields of rapidly changing winds, temperature, and moisture. Old debates will be resolved, new ones will supersede them, and more questions will undoubtedly be posed. Someday, the seed of pure research is expected to bear practical fruit through improved tornado warnings and forecasts.

Another legacy of VORTEX and the professional storm-chasing movement is already evident in a thrilling new hobby on the High Plains. A small and dogged group of amateurs and freelancers think nothing of driving all day simply to view and film tornadoes. As some Oklahomans scurry for the cellar, they point the nose of their cars at the area under the black heart of the storm and stomp on the gas pedal. For anyone who truly loves weather, storm chasing is definitely an unforgettable experience.

10

Tornado on the Ground!

It's a warm day in May, the peak month for tornadoes in Oklahoma, but storm chaser Greg Stumpf scowls as he peers over the steering wheel. A dull quilt of low clouds extends to the west, seemingly forever. "This is sort of disheartening, to see the clouds are so thick," he says as we slip into the traffic stream on the interstate. He's discouraged, but at the same time hopeful that somewhere out there, where skies are clear and the sun is baking the ground, a severe thunderstorm will fire up later.

For those who know how to read them, the red-flag signs are waving. Dew points over the region are high enough to support deep cloud growth, and the atmosphere is unstable, just waiting for a good jolt to get things going. Satellite pictures show, far off to our west, a skinny thread of north-south clouds marking a dryline that runs from west Texas through Oklahoma. Some of the most breathtaking storms on Earth form along drylines.

"There are incredible instabilities," Greg confirms with guarded optimism. He stifles a yawn and shifts his six-four, 210-pound frame in the bucket seat of his Honda CRX. He was wrestling until 2:30 A.M. with a radar algorithm to detect tornado-spawning mesocyclones, a project he's working on as a research meteorologist for the National Severe Storms Laboratory.

At first glance, Greg might be mistaken for a surfer: big boned, good looking, sandy brown hair feathered long in back. But the last time Oklahoma saw ocean waters was some 65 million years ago, and he speaks an arcane lingo that no West Coast beach worshiper would understand. It's peppered with

references to "bounded weak-echo regions," "shear zones," and
"triple points." At 28, he's already a veteran of some 170 storm
chases or so. He ditches work for the afternoon, sometimes to
stumble home at two in the morning with nothing more to show
for his efforts than a sunburn.

As we leave Oklahoma City on west-running Interstate 40,
the thick clouds continue to stretch to the horizon. Iron-rich red
Permian clay shines with recent rain and young wheat stalks
bend low before a strong south wind. Behind us, a rented cherry-
red Hyundai follows at an even distance. Inside are brothers Bill
and Tom Oosterbaan, weather lovers in their late 30s who are on
vacation and in hopes of following Greg right to the vortex.

Bill and Tom have tracked a few storms in their home state
of Michigan. They fit the storm chaser profile: weather junkies,
20 to 40 years old, male. This hobby attracts a lot of men. It's a
tactical enterprise (map-reading skills are critical for a successful
intercept), a trophy-bagging expedition (film images serve as a
tornado surrogate), and a high-adrenalin sport. Yet you can't
assume too much about storm chasers because enthusiasts have
included doctors and lawyers, a meat plant owner, a data
transcriber, and even a couple of Dominican priests.

They're all patient gamblers. They have to be. The romantic
phrase "chasing the wind" suggests a certain absurdity, even
futility, but time and again they take the gamble to wager their
forecasting smarts and instincts. Surely, I think to myself, no
one would fathom this in the small New England town I grew up
in. Weather was a quiet bit player in the drama of our lives. Fog
wreathed knolls and winter storms glazed bare tree limbs with
ice. Weather wasn't supposed to kill, not with sudden fury. We
greeted news of a rare tornado watch on a hot August day with
curiosity and disbelief. No one really expected to see anything. In
Oklahoma they count the steps to the shelter. Or gas up the
Honda and pack the cameras and filters and lenses for a weather
safari.

At 3:20 P.M., Greg stops at a Texaco service station to stretch
out, buy chips and soda, and top off the tank. Finding a perfect
tornado in perfect lighting is no good if the gas needle sinks
below E. Back on the road, he nurses a Diet Mountain Dew,
clearly impatient. "Our best bet is to continue on," he says. "You

waste too much time doing stuff like this." "Stuff like this" includes eating a sit-down meal, stopping to use the bathroom,
anything but stalking the storm. Of course we don't have one yet,
which is really what annoys him.

Storm chasers like to swap stories to pass the time, and Greg
tells me about April 26, 1991, the last big outbreak across the
Southern Plains. A full week in advance, weather forecasters
could see big trouble coming. Early that afternoon, the National
Severe Storms Forecast Center slapped tornado watch boxes
from northern Oklahoma up through Nebraska. Before day's
end, 54 twisters had touched down.

The most deadly one whirled through Kansas and, depending on who you asked, sounded like a giant vacuum cleaner, low-
flying jets, hundreds of clattering skateboards, or a space shuttle
launch. It looked to an eyewitness like a wheeling flock of thousands of black birds. The twister crossed the Kansas Turnpike in
south Wichita, briefly turning pink after inhaling geraniums
from a greenhouse.

It left behind a scattering of wreckage and a string of narrow
escapes. A staff sergeant at an Air Force base slid low into a cast-
iron bathtub with his cocker spaniel on his chest. His duplex
broke up, and the tub snapped free of the pipes. It spun around
like a freakish carnival ride before shooting out the front door
and flipping, trapping him for a while underneath. He wasn't
seriously injured, and neither were two sisters who emerged a
little prematurely from their basement shelter. Thinking the
danger had passed, each then happened to look out different
windows. One saw a bright rainbow. The other was looking
straight at a tornado. They dashed back to the basement before
it slammed into the house.

Some didn't escape at the Golden Spur Mobile Home Park in
the town of Andover. Taking comfort in a glimpse of sunshine at
the horizon, they ignored storm warnings and sirens. And 11
paid with their lives. The tornado smeared the mobile home
park, Greg says somberly. That is the sight he'll never forget.

He was part of a group that went to Andover the day after, to
do an official damage survey. They drove by a fast-food restaurant with minor damage, and some telephone poles blown down.
To their left was a big junkyard. That junkyard turned out to be
the Golden Spur trailer park.

"Completely blended," Greg says, awed, as if seeing it again. Blended. Chewed up, spit out, chewed up. If you're going to chase storms, he thinks, you need to get that close to the shocking aftermath at least once to know what a tornado can do.

We have exited the interstate, onto a patchwork of rougher roads leading into northwestern Oklahoma. They run alongside straight railroad tracks and wide pastures, and through lone towns untouched by time and strangely somnolent at midday. "Boaters are advised to stay off lakes today," warns the radio. Standing water ripples in ditches.

The miles pile up, the towns blur.

"A storm chaser has to get used to a lot of driving," Greg muses. "For ten minutes of glory." For four years he's been seeking that glory in his Honda, chaser accessorized down to the RAIN-X on the windshield. RAIN-X creates a clear, waxy film that causes raindrops to ball up and skitter away like tiny BBs. The product's advertising boasts of making glass so slippery that rain, sleet, snow, frost, bugs, mud, or salt spray can hardly stick to it.

Unfortunately, there's nothing called HAIL-X to guarantee you'll still have a windshield to look through. Greg's car roof has so much bonding compound holding it together, he quips that he can barely attach his two magnetic antennas. In two separate episodes, hail damage to the car totaled $1,100 and $1,400. In fairness, only one bill resulted from a storm chase. What a day: hail smashed the windshield, split the plastic housing for the side-view mirror, web-cracked the mirror inside, broke a parking light, and dimpled the metal body. Greg hastens to point out that he did see three tornadoes.

Hail can kill. I'm reminded of a historical account reprinted in the magazine *Stormtrack*. On a July day in 1545, an artist by the name of Benvenuto Cellini was traveling on horseback from Paris to Florence. Thunder grumbled in the clear blue sky. He heard a terrible noise from high above. Hail, "larger than chalk balls from an air gun," began to fall. Cellini galloped on his frightened horse to some pine trees under which his companions were taking shelter. The hailstones, getting larger by the second, were the size of lemons. He sang a miserere, or prayer for mercy, only to be interrupted by a lump of hail that snapped the huge branch he was hiding under. Another struck his horse in the head, almost knocking it down. Realizing that prayer alone might not save him, Cellini swathed his head in his garments.

The hailstorm passed and the bruised men resumed their journey. Only a mile away they came upon "a scene of ruin which it is impossible to describe." Trees were stripped of branches, and beasts and shepherds were sprawled about, dead. The hailstones, Cellini reported, were too large for two hands to span them. If true, this would make them bigger than softballs. Such hail is very rare, though dimensions range from the mundane (dime or pea sized) to the eye opening (golf ball or baseball sized) to the terrifying (softball or grapefruit sized).

As I wonder how a windshield would shatter, a radio announcer on the government-operated weather channel runs through a list of temperatures. Greg listens closely. Woodward is 73, and a little to its south, it's 85 in Childress, Texas. He explains that this means sun in Childress, too many clouds in Woodward. Childress, or some nearby town, could be the storm's birthing ground.

On our approach to Watonga, I admire a majestic butte with dark red earth spilling off its steep sides. Greg agrees, but establishes our priorities, adding, "As long as that's not blocking the tornado view." He doesn't pretend to be carrying Nikon and Pentax 35-millimeter cameras, and a "monster tripod" that can withstand 50-mile-an-hour winds, just to photograph beautiful outcroppings. He likes the flatness of western Oklahoma precisely for the superior viewing.

On an open stretch of road, we have our first brush with danger. An oncoming sports coupe swings out wide to pass a car, then cuts back jerkily into its own lane with only seconds to spare. The common wisdom is that driving poses a much bigger threat than anything the storm flings at you. Only one person has died doing this, a 21-year-old University of Oklahoma sophomore. In April of 1984 he lost control of his Mazda, apparently after swerving to avoid a rabbit on a rain-slicked road.

The deeper we penetrate the native prairie, the fewer cars and people we meet. Beyond graying fence posts strung with miles of barbed wire are sparse and stubby evergreens presiding over an ocean of grass. "Jesus is Lord of Nelson Ranch," announces a roadside sign. In Seiling the signs boast of being the hometown of TV weatherman Gary England. Greg, a longtime piano player and former New Yorker, slips in a cassette tape of original keyboard compositions that has a quirky, bright feel, incongruous with our surroundings. Leaving Seiling, he leans on the gas. Winds are raking the fields, which he notes favorably.

Just after 4:30 P.M. we catch a break. A tornado watch goes out over the radio for extreme northwestern Oklahoma. Greg scrambles to grab his tape recorder and makes an entry. After clicking it off, in a quiet, pleased voice he says, "Good. Now I'm happy." Should the chase fail, at least we share poor judgment with the forecasters in Kansas City. On an AM radio station, bursts of static indicate lightning, somewhere. Greg hopefully mentions "six o'clock magic," when tornadoes are supposed to drop and dance. It seems possible, for the sun is now visible above low clouds rushing about. Dust scatters across the road in 25-mile-an-hour gusts.

Greg's forecasting skill has brought us this far, but with a watch box out, we need to monitor better breaking developments. Since he's limited in a car to what he sees through the windshield and hears on radio bands, Greg likes to phone co-workers at NSSL for the latest weather satellite and ground radar observations. Before doing that, he has to nail down the boundaries of the watch box. At a gas station he calls another storm chaser, who delivers bad news. The weather service seems to be hedging its bets. The watch area is tall and thin, stretching to the Rio Grande at the Mexican border, some 450 miles away. We revise our route to the southwest, and off we race.

Despair begins to settle in. Greg's exuberance upon hearing of the tornado watch is gone. Some dark-bellied clouds in the distance fail to cheer him. He sighs. He wants a total clearing, then firm towers shooting up, all alone. We zip past an old concrete storm bunker overgrown with weeds, the red Hyundai still matching us, mile for mile. Crossing into the Texas Panhandle, we're doing 65 and dodging gaping potholes. The terrain is even flatter. Besides a rare stand of trees, and an oil rig pumping in a languorous rhythm, there's nothing but the clouds. Which aren't too impressive.

"The low clouds look the same as back in Oklahoma," Greg complains.

He swears.

And then a tiny break in the bland whiteness reveals a distant high rosy peak, like a mountain summit glimpsed through the fog. It's a heaped cumulonimbus catching the sun's late-afternoon rays. Hope surges—at last, something promising. A roadrunner darts in front of the car, disappearing on quick, pencil-thin legs. On the country radio station we've tuned to for weather bulletins, a singer pines in a mournful bass, "Last night I dug your picture out of the dresser drawer, I set it on the table, I talked to it until four." We notice the Hyundai is following too closely.

That puzzles us until we pull over to consult our maps, to figure out where to proceed. Bill leaps out of their car. "There's an F4 on the ground!" he shouts, panting. We've been listening to the wrong radio station. We spin out in a big cloud of dust, the map in my lap, Greg's hands tight on the steering wheel. The tornado has been sighted to our north. A man with a deep, steady voice on our new radio station is tracking it: "A tornado warning is in effect for Texas County. The tornado is located right now near the Hitch headquarters. Hardesty is in the path of this storm. They're getting ready to blow the sirens."

We near the southeast flank of the storm. We're coming in from the southeast so Greg can photograph a dark tornado against a light, rainfree background. And we're coming in from the southeast, he reminds me, so we don't get clobbered. We'll have "east options," roads to scoot down if a tornado unexpectedly turns on us. Suddenly the chilling reality fully sinks in, that we're pursuing a type of storm that forms swiftly and behaves erratically—and that could, in an instant, knot a car like his around a telephone pole.

The radio signal abruptly vanishes. Maybe lightning has knocked the station off the air. On our approach to Guymon, lightning shimmers deep in the storm cloud, like distant artillery flashes on a smoke-obscured battlefield. The whole scene is strange. To the south, untroubled blue skies reign, then to the north, a hazy purple cowl covers the flank of this gray colossus skimming low over the ground. It has a backsheared anvil formed by updraft winds so intense that, instead of flowing downwind with the rest of the anvil, they shove upstream against the prevailing current.

"Oh my goodness, this thing is a bell," Greg marvels. Its trunk is shaped like a bell spun on a potter's wheel. As we drive north, parallel to the storm, we see sharp, riblike striations along its bulky middle revealing the rotation. To our east, small tattered clouds stream in through clear skies. Their moisture is continuously converted to energy, like kindling for a fire. To our west, the storm looms darkly, in brooding pewter.

Buried in there is a white shadowy snake, which Greg excitedly identifies as a tornado. It makes a brief appearance and can be seen only with difficulty. Over the scanner, spotters confirm that the tornado has roped out. Our scanner's weak batteries won't last much longer. Then again, if a fresh wall cloud keeps lowering, they won't have to.

"There's the rearflank downdraft," Greg triumphantly exclaims.

He points out a clear slot yawning in the cloud, where cool air rushing off the rear of the mesocyclone has tumbled from great heights and eroded a hole. At least one theory of how a tornado forms assigns a pivotal role to the rearflank downdraft. It's clear why as a slender V begins its descent nearby. Dirt flies up below the still lowering funnel, marking the touchdown. Tornado on the ground!

It strengthens and widens to a thick gray wedge, pulsing and boiling with energy. Greg parks at the mouth of a dirt section road. Melting hailstones glisten in the mud. Wind rattles the louvers over the hatchback's rear window, and we take turns opening our doors, so as not to lose any loose maps. We step into a warm, damp breeze, feeling powerfully exhilarated. A surreal shade of silvery green glows on the table-flat land. Ordinarily the wandering eye would not find an object to rest on out here. But not today.

Bill and Tom spill out of their car, camcorder at the ready. "Only 20 percent ground," Greg yells over the rushing wind. The other 80 percent of the camera frame is reserved for the main attraction, the action in the sky. Greg, the collar of his teal polo shirt snapping up, sets up his tripod in the soupy mud and complains about the scarce light. From out of nowhere a tumbleweed somersaults past, bouncing off to a rendezvous with the twister. Birds fly up, then swoop back down and stay low, out of the worst of the brisk winds flowing into the thunderstorm.

"Turn the autofocus off and put the video recorder on infinity," Greg hollers.

That clinches what this must be, something beyond our ken like the concept of infinity. It's atmospheric physics gone haywire, a frightening revelation of order buried in dull chaos. Clouds just aren't supposed to be able to do this. And when you look at this thing, spinning and black, you feebly drop your arms at your sides and your skin crawls. For that moment of immediacy, you don't try to figure it out; some visions are simply irreducible. You watch it, respect it. The sky has boldly embraced the earth and inverted the natural order of things. How could anyone have seen this centuries ago and not bolted in terror?

We cannot hear the tornado, which is a bit disturbing. A novice might be tempted to pull closer, but not Greg. Before we pulled over he warned, only half joking, "Let's make sure that it doesn't eat us." This is no movie; no screen separates us from what is churning only several miles west. At least it's "translating," or moving to the right of our frame of reference. When a tornado just grows larger, a smart storm chaser packs up the gear and gets out fast, because it's coming right at him. This one continues on its northward track, and Greg folds up the tripod and we climb back into the car.

We cross into Kansas from the Oklahoma Panhandle. The storm streaks 35, 40 miles an hour, roughly parallel to the highway, dragging the tornado with it. We're safe unless the twister lurches right—which is not uncommon. Just in case, I plan escape routes on a road map, one of many in a thick blue binder. Each page is a map sheet, sheathed in plastic so that storm paths and watch boxes can be sketched directly on with an erasable marker. Greg logs entries on the tape recorder, preceding descriptions of the changing tornado with the mileage and time. A Kansas highway patrol car hurtles past, bubble light flashing. That sense of urgency is contrasted with the chasers we're now seeing, standing calmly outside with cameras aimed at the storm.

Tornado witnessed by author on May 5, 1993. *Bill and Tom Oosterbaan*

They have to hurry. A rain curtain is wrapping around the funnel. The blurry, gray veil looks like a cylindrical elevator closing. We stop to watch in the fading twilight. While the old tornado weakens, to its northeast strengthens a wall cloud from which dip dark, ragged tongues. Two adjacent tornadoes seldom both live, in competition. And so, a once vigorous whirl slims to a thick rope while, under the new wall cloud, a shaggy nub struggles lower. The first one gives it up. It narrows, seems to freeze, then dissolves into dozens of pieces like a snake hacked with a machete. From the new wall cloud a fresh tornado touches ground.

Greg eases out, tires crunching over pea-sized hail on the wet road. We pursue, but not for long. It's too hard to make out the tornado's location by lightning flashes. Rather than risk stumbling into its path, Greg rolls in behind three cars parked along the road. Only a muddy pink wash remains of the sunset.

We join the others standing outside, fondly watching the retreating lightning. A University of Oklahoma student in a weather-themed cartoon T-shirt notes that some fellow students missed this because of a meteorology final exam. We mull the irony. Greg keeps glancing directly overhead. He's worried about an anticyclonic tornado—which rotates clockwise instead of counterclockwise—forming right over our heads.

That we have become separated from Bill and Tom I don't realize until a red, mud-spattered car pulls up. Breaking a cardinal rule of storm chasing, they took a dirt back road. Unpaved roads are generally avoided because they're slippery, impassable if flooded, and sometimes abruptly end in washed-out bridges. Bright-eyed and incredulous, the brothers tell their story, of how the car slewed in the mud as they neared the tornado, of how a farmer in the middle of a cornfield matter-of-factly watched it go by. They stopped to do some videotaping, and Tom happened to look straight up into a rotating cloud feeding down tendrils. A moment later, the Hyundai was sliding down the road again, pointed in the other direction.

Happily tired, we trade stories, then set out under a milk-white moon for a Dodge City motel. Headlights wash over leaves and small branches strewn over the road, the edge of the storm's damage footprint. At a closed gas station with a pay phone, again we congregate with other chasers.

"The contrast was kind of rough," a serious-looking bearded Texan says quietly, in an almost reverential whisper. "It was a very beautiful updraft, nice striations."

But it didn't hit anything, someone complains.

"Where's a good 10-story building when you need one?"

When we are alone, Greg makes clear that he does not like the image that such comments contribute to, that of storm chasers as disaster vultures. For him today was perfect, tornadoes hitting nothing but wheat. Still, it's hard to shake off that remark. In a way we all seem guilty, in wishing for a tornado, then wanting the monster to prove what it can do. And then we drive away. Others can't.

The Dodge City motel is pleasant enough, cheap but clean. The rooms lack cable, keenly disappointing Greg. No Weather Channel. We retire early and sleep well, then in the morning toss on our unwashed clothes from the day before. Outside, a dry, brisk wind greets us. At the motel greasy spoon we heap on our plates bacon, scrambled eggs, and link sausage, all coated with the same glistening sheen. "Triple-bypass breakfast," Greg remarks cheerfully.

At our booth, he tests his artistic skills, sketching with a blue marker on a place mat the outline of a classic mesocyclonic storm. It looks like half of a yin-yang symbol, but could be a curvaceous nude, the way Bill admires it. Greg stabs the marker at where an anticyclonic tornado could have formed yesterday.

"I'm hooked," Bill exults. "This is going to become an annual pilgrimage to Mecca."

It's almost as if Bill and Tom are reliving their boyhoods. Bill is a small-business owner and Tom a social worker, but once they return to Michigan, I suspect that at work they'll be preoccupied, doodling tightly coiled cones on message pads.

Checking out of the motel, we notice a message frozen beside the soap opera figures on the office TV set: "Severe t-storm warning/Logan County/Until 11:15 A.M." It looks active early. For better intelligence, we drive out to the Dodge City National Weather Service office, a modern building easily identifiable by the white ball of a Doppler radar perched out front.

Greg smoothly talks his way in, swapping a detailed tornado log he made yesterday for a fax just sent over from the county fire chief's office. In a straightforward, just-the-facts style, the fire chief reports that the tornado was half a mile wide, traveled more than 25 miles, and destroyed a farmstead, two irrigation sprinkler systems, and a garage. Miraculously, it caused no deaths and only a minor injury.

It's quiet and empty here, nothing like what it must have been like at eight o'clock the evening before. On long, crescent-shaped desks facing each other, terminals display brightly colored radar images of storms already on the rampage. At a special terminal, his fingers flicking over the keyboard, Greg calls up severe weather information. Tornado watches have an enhanced warning: "This is a particularly dangerous situation with the possibility of very damaging tornadoes." It's only noon, and the alarm bells are pealing furiously.

By 1 P.M., we're driving under a dome of luxurious deep blue and gazing east at craggy, snow-white clouds soaring on the moist edge of a dryline. We want to position ourselves farther east, so as not to be trapped under thunderstorms if they pop up. Storm chasers love drylines. From the hot, dry air on the west side of this boundary to the warm, moist air less than two miles east, the dew point—a measurement of moisture in the air—can leap more than 30 degrees. Drylines occur on almost half the days in spring over this region. They slosh back and forth for a few days, advancing by day and retreating by night before disappearing altogether.

Drylines are so beloved because they're accidents waiting to happen. If one bulges at some point along its length, a low-pressure area can form. The swirling low draws in lots of damp air, the fuel for an embryonic cumulonimbus. That's one way to create a dryline storm, which is famous for being fierce and crisply picturesque, its features standing out in high relief. Such a storm tends to be isolated as well.

Once we move a good 30 miles ahead of the dryline, we swing into a gas station to watch and wait. Today will be an early show, Greg predicts. A snapping wind stings our bare legs with fine dirt. Bill squints into the sun, pensively chewing on a ham-and-cheese sandwich.

"We got spoiled yesterday," he reflects. "Drive up and do it and watch it go down and drive to the motel."

A pretty young Hispanic woman in a black satin jacket steps out of a silver sedan. She flashes a brilliant smile at us, four unshaven men in wrinkled and unwashed clothes, then eases into a spiel, something about being from Dallas and discount surplus cologne, 50 to 80 percent off. We pass on the offer and wait some more. Before long, a familiar car crunches in over the dusty parking lot. Aboard are other storm chasers, including Herbert Fiala, a 45-year-old Viennese aviation meteorologist. He's good humored and talkative, with a gleam in his eye. Does the Austrian capital ever have tornadoes? Fiala shakes his head. "It could happen, but it would be the event of the century." So he finds his adventure—where else?—in Tornado Alley. Fiala wryly observes that the wind inflow into the supercell yesterday was paralleled on the ground by a storm-chaser inflow.

The sun sinks a little lower. Greg decides to continue east, but uncertainly. We don't know exactly where to go. It doesn't help that the dryline has jumped. He explains that it doesn't have to be like a moving wall, stretching miles straight up. There can be a dryline at the surface, then another aloft to its east, mixing out with moist air below. What results is the disorganized mess we see before us. Puny, uninteresting cumulus float by.

We bypass Wichita, Kansas, on the interstate, then the radio reports a tornado southwest of Topeka, more than one hundred miles north. We can't catch that storm, but Greg has me plot on a map our hypothetical intersection with a rotating thunderstorm barreling across the Oklahoma border. We close in on our new objective, then spy the tip of a faraway crenulated tower burnished pink. That's our supercell. Then, in keeping with the day's luck, we get stuck at a railway crossing on the wrong side of a long train. Car after car clacks by.

"Perfect timing," Greg says. "If we miss the tornado by three minutes . . ."

It doesn't matter. A law officer on the scanner describes the storm as "showing signs of falling apart."

"Oh no," Greg despairs.

And so, the vortex eludes us on day two. On the long drive back, Greg tries to relax, but the sky is full of temptations.

"Hey. What the heck is going on over there?" he asks in southeastern Kansas, his head swivelling sharply around.

Further examination is discouraging.

"Nah," he says. "It's a joke."

Just God teasing an addled storm chaser.

But being a devotee of this hobby means never giving up, because if you do, you'll probably miss the Big One. No one wants to risk having to watch the F5 tornado of the decade on the evening news from the living room sofa. So when Gene Rhoden calls the very next morning with only one question—do I want to go?—half a minute later, I'm tossing a clean T-shirt and a toothbrush in an overnight bag.

At the National Severe Storms Laboratory, Gene is aching to leave. A cup anemometer twirls high over the rear bumper of his shiny black van, and the videotape camera mounted behind the dashboard adds a professional touch. Gene is a meteorology student at the University of Oklahoma, thin and angular in build, with a piercing, serious gaze. He measures his words carefully, as when he softly predicts that a little cumulus cloud is going to spin out of control today. As we move quickly out of Norman, once again toward northwestern Oklahoma, the National Weather Service echoes his assessment. The early radio reports warn that we're driving into a "dangerous, life-threatening severe weather situation." In a thunderstorm, the van's high profile is a mixed blessing, Gene informs me. The vehicle is more susceptible to tipping in a strong wind gust, but on the plus side, can more easily ford streams that overrun the roadway.

A few hours later, on the outskirts of Woodward, we get a look at a tantalizing prospect. We are standing calf deep in roadside grass with *Stormtrack* editor Tim Marshall, handsome and square jawed and nonchalant about a television crew, doing a documentary, hanging avidly on his every word and gesture. A swelling cloud to the northwest throws up muscular towers with abandon. Meanwhile, to our rear, a filmy anvil edges in. Decision time: the storm to the north, the storm to the south.

"Eenie meenie minie moe," Tim says loudly, a smile flickering around the corners of his mouth. "Which one?"

Yellow-and-black Santa Fe Railway cars rumble in the foreground below the cumulonimbus to our north, which would draw us into Kansas. Behind us, its pale purple anvil throwing down a chilly gloom, is a great unknown. Tim flips a quarter. Heads north, tails south. It's tails.

The decision made, Gene and I wistfully backtrack across Woodward. We know what we had; we don't know what we're getting. Circling the new storm, we view the anvil thrusting over town. A slot in the body of the cloud opens onto a dusky yellow chamber, like a secret grotto that gods might caper in.

As we proceed south, fat drops of rain splatter the windshield. In a small town, a boy on a neon-green bicycle gawks at our convoy, bristling with tall whip antennas and rushing along with a singular purpose. Preoccupied, Gene doesn't notice. He's worried about thunderstorms that, according to the radio, are firing up everywhere.

"Hate it if it goes up all over the place," he mutters anxiously.

This sounds paradoxical, a storm chaser who doesn't want storms. But the problem is, they thrive in isolation. Populate an area with a litter of small storms and they compete with each other for moisture. No single one grows into a dominant giant. A radio report out of Woodward describes a possibly developing tornado obscured by rain, no good for us. We separate from Marshall and his entourage, who are inclined to move south and deeper into Texas, his home base. Our options look poor all over. Not so long ago, the day seemed perfect, a matter of picking storms like candy from a tray, but the atmosphere has overturned too quickly, in too many places. Hearing of a tornado near a town to our south, we bolt down there, only to discover a sorry-looking, flaking wall cloud. Lightning arcs around the rim. It looks like a piece of chewed-up meat.

"This is all dead," Gene says dully. "No updraft left."

We make our way toward the twinkling night lights of Elk City, then home on I-40, trying to figure out what went wrong. Usually something does. Later I learn from Tim Marshall what qualifies as a "good" year. In 1989, according to his meticulous records, he averaged 512 miles and 11.1 hours per outing. And for what? One tornado every 10 trips. That equals driving coast to coast across the United States, then halfway back again. For a glimpse at one tornado.

As dismal as that seems, the real hard luck story goes back to the 1950s, before the existence of sophisticated storm-probing equipment and dependable tornado forecasts. No one chased after storms. No one thought to. Then a kid from Bismarck, North Dakota, fell under the spell of the tempest and blazed a trail for others to follow. To grasp the history of amateur storm chasing, to understand why dozens of cars fan out over Oklahoma each spring at the crack of thunder, you have to start farther north. From there, you meet a whole gallery of hardcore weather freaks with one driving passion and many stories of big days and close encounters.

11

Storm Fever

At some point, serious tornado researchers had little choice but to pursue their subject. They needed direct observations and close-up measurements to understand a nearly inaccessible enigma. Perhaps this sense of purpose and duty explained why the wonder and awe they felt always seemed incidental to their mission. In the accounts of field expeditions they wrote up for professional journals, any trace of emotion was expunged. From the flat tone of their careful, objective prose, a reader might have thought that they were analyzing rock stratifications or specifying gene-marker locations, and not relating firsthand encounters with the most terrifying storm on the planet.

For better or for worse, amateur storm chasers have no such inhibitions. In their ranks, a feeling of excitement has always been freely expressed and duly acknowledged. They speak of a fever that grips them in spring as days lengthen and a warm, wet wind begins to flow out of the south. They measure each other by depth of passion. A nickname bandied about is "gentleman chaser"—a derisive label applied to those dilettantes interested in tracking only storms within an easy drive.

Passion marked the true hobbyist right from the beginning. Nothing else but this intense drive could explain a man like Dave Hoadley, who is known as the father of the amateur storm chase. He was the original Ironman, investing 70,000 miles over six years before seeing his first tornado. He undertook this quest at the tender age of 17, before which he paid hardly any attention to the weather, except as it provided an opportunity to fly

his kite. He still remembers clearly one fateful June night in
1956 in his hometown of Bismarck, North Dakota.

"I went downtown to the movies, the early evening show. I
was in there about 30 minutes and I could hear thunder, very
loud. My dad came down the aisle to where I was sitting. He
tapped me on the shoulder and said, 'There's a better show outside.' So we left the theater. At that point the storm had almost
completely passed over the city. There was light rainfall and the
streets were overrunning with water. I was impressed by how
things had changed. I saw large cottonwood trees, so large you
couldn't put your arms around them, pulled out by the roots. I
saw electrical lines dancing in the grass, sparking, arcing, bouncing around."

The next day, armed with an eight-millimeter camera,
Hoadley roamed around and made a record of the damage. His
curiosity was piqued, and he buttonholed local meteorologists to
query them about storms. Then he began to borrow the family
Oldsmobile to attempt to photograph thunderheads. He often
found himself on the road working a desperate math in his head:
if it was 70 miles away, moving off at 30 miles an hour, and he
drove 60, he could catch it in only . . . two hours or so. Frustration dogged him at every turn. He either was trapped behind
motorists crawling down rural two-lane highways or reached
promising towers that collapsed and spent their waning life
gushing rain.

Had his father known about the degree of futility involved,
he might not have been so concerned about his son's being spirited away by a tornado. That was a very slim possibility. In the
late 1950s, both the Weather Bureau and young Dave Hoadley
were neophytes of a sort—the weather agency in making accurate, precise tornado forecasts, Hoadley in knowing how to properly chase a thunderstorm.

Despite a run of poor luck, failure never diminished his
eagerness. He restlessly anticipated each June, the beginning of
the brief severe weather season in North Dakota. After graduat-
ing from college, he joined ROTC and was asked where he
wanted to do basic training. Everyone else chose exotic, popular
locales. He stunned his superiors by requesting Fort Riley, Kansas. Why hot, desolate Fort Riley? Oh, he had an interest there,

Hoadley said mysteriously, and spent off-duty weekends running after Kansas storms. Even marriage and a career move to take a position with the Environmental Protection Agency as a budget analyst in Washington, D.C., didn't deter Hoadley from partaking of his favorite activity. Each spring he returned to the Great Plains to rekindle what had become for him a romance. He was a common sight at far-flung weather offices, a clipboard in hand on which to jot down and plot out fresh weather data. Hoadley, a nonmeteorologist, used a complicated forecasting method of his own devising that baffled even senior forecasters. He was unfailingly gracious and always had a storm photo or two, tucked in his sheaf of papers, to share with the crew on duty. He traded pleasantries, but always with an eye stealing over to the clock. If he left late, he would sometimes forgo lunch to reach his target area for the day.

Hoadley was a private man, one of those private men whose polite exteriors throw up an inoffensive shield to their real desires. He enjoyed the beauty of the plains and traveling in solitude, imagining the land he crossed in an earlier era, alive with wagon schooners and Indian tribal dances. He would have been perfectly happy being the lone storm chaser, eating his peanut butter-and-cheese crackers in his car late at night and belting out Western ballads to stay awake, then checking into a motel in a city he might never pass through again. But like it or not, Hoadley was more often crossing the paths of other like-minded enthusiasts. The National Severe Storms Laboratory unwittingly ensured as much with the publicized accomplishments of its Tornado Intercept Project.

The amount of interest surprised him at a 1977 severe storms conference in Omaha, Nebraska. He consented to allow the organizers to decorate a back wall with dozens of his prints of tornadoes, wall clouds, mammatus, and towering cumulus. Conference goers spent much time ranging along that wall, admiring his work. When they approached him to buy copies of certain prints, the unprepared Hoadley had to grab a blank sheet of paper and scribble down names and addresses for orders.

Upon further reflection, he decided the time had come to

unite the storm-chasing community. December 31, 1977, marked the date of the first issue of *Stormtrack*, a bimonthly newsletter. Hoadley wrote and edited the contents and stapled together pages for all 18 copies of the maiden issue. *Stormtrack* became a forum for a small and free-spirited bunch of individuals who, at the end of each spring, tended to scatter to the same winds they had come to follow. It captured the flavor and thrill of the chase, and on its pages, Hoadley indulged a fondness for both musing and amusing. His cartoons in clean lines revealed a droll, inventive wit. In one, a dead storm chaser's ashes are offered up solemnly to wind flowing into a wall cloud. He made light of their collective obsession, but then sought reasons for it in more contemplative moments, wondering why "an unknown destiny drives me on."

By the mid-1980s, *Stormtrack* counted 176 subscribers in 34 states, Washington, D.C., Canada, and Guam. It was no accident that the popularity of storm chasing spiked upward at the same time a device was being mass marketed that in years to come would be a cliche at children's birthday parties and wedding receptions: the camcorder. It revolutionized that part of the hobby that was about returning with tangible proof of success. A photograph reproduced only a static slice of time. A videotape vaulted the viewer onto a startling new level of intimacy. All of a sudden there was the tornado, too close for comfort, seen out a rear car window through a bobbling lens while scared voices cursed and doors slammed.

This could be exciting stuff on the written page as well. In 1983, *The Atlantic Monthly* dispatched writer Bill Hauptman to accompany some storm-chasing meteorologists from NSSL. Their expedition was almost too successful. They saw one tornado at close range and, parked in the dark, had their van rocked by a 65-mile-an-hour wind. Next spring, Hauptman's article appeared under the title "On the Dryline."

He brought a special perspective to the piece. As a child in the 1950s, he possessed an almost crippling fear of tornadoes. Raised in Wichita Falls, Texas, just south of the Oklahoma border, he was quite familiar with them at an early age. He was about eight when he saw a very small tornado cross a vacant lot at the end of his block. The red, whirling dust column against the storm's dark rain shaft was harmless, but he panicked. He left his parents in the backyard and ran across the street, crying, and begged a woman to let him into her storm cellar. His mother and father disapproved of his phobia, so he spoke little of it. One time he was riding back from Austin with his mother, his father trailing behind in a just purchased used car. Kneeling on the front seat, he looked over his mother's shoulder at an approaching storm. There it was, as he knew it would be, in front of a bright, clear slot in the clouds. The tornado closed in and blew across the road, almost pushing his father into the ditch. He said nothing.

Then, following a psychological pattern familiar to many storm chasers, the advent of adolescence transformed his dread into high excitement. Storms stoked his passion. He took girlfriends in his 1957 Chevrolet to a dead-end road on a cliff overlooking the Wichita River. As rain sheeted off the hood and windows, and thunder cracked wetly, he felt thrilled to be in the presence of such power.

His writing for *The Atlantic* drew on this welter of strong, conflicting emotions. The paralyzing childhood fear resurfaced at times, along with a keen sense of exhilaration. After fulfilling his journalistic obligation for the magazine, he could have shelved his old nightmares once and for all. But he didn't. Instead, he occasionally went storm chasing with his younger brother Tom, who once had tornado nightmares that threw him into sheet-soaking sweats. Tom had good reason to be scared. He barely outran the famous mile-wide killer Wichita Falls tornado of 1979, racing across town with his family in the car, the roaring funnel at his heels.

As a writer, Bill Hauptman was fascinated by the psyche of the storm chaser, the complicated psychological attraction to violent weather, and the sublime beauty of the tornado. "When you see a tornado form, the cloud at that point is circulating so rapidly, it's like time-lapse photography. It's like relativity. It's an awesome sight because you're seeing something that is ordinarily not visible; you're seeing high-energy physics. You know you're seeing a miracle." He found a vehicle for his thoughts in *The Storm Season*, a novel he wrote about an aspiring musician mired in a life of vague malcontent in a small Texas town. Being in the presence of storms galvanizes and focuses the main character in existential clarity. Storms are a symbol for revitalization, physical and spiritual.

Today, seekers of meaning and thrills all fit into the fast-expanding ranks of what Hauptman likes to call "an environmental thrill sport." Thousands of dollars are invested to outfit the perfect vehicle. A customized "chasemobile" does not come cheap. Its contents include everything from a compass, scanner, ham radio, portable television, and assorted still and video cameras to a laptop computer, cellular phone, and a raft of instruments to measure the immediate atmosphere. Some consider having this much equipment de rigueur, but others hunt twisters in almost anything that rolls down the highway.

Pat Foster of Midwest City, Oklahoma, has adopted a simple, no-frills style. On his jaunts, he consults an ordinary state road map and, in place of meteorology training, has developed a simple rule of thumb: Drive straight at the most intense cluster of lightning. It has worked. He's seen tornadoes, and has been directly under rotating wall clouds and felt his stomach flip queasily and his ears ache from the low pressure. Foster, who has lank brown hair and an easy smile, had an unnerving near miss once.

"I had WKY radio on, it gave good bulletins. I intercepted a tornado just north of Shawnee. It was a mile south, moving due east like me, so I followed it for two or three miles. It was the mid-1970s, not many chasers back then. We were hopscotching down the road—I'd drive a quarter mile, pull over, somebody would pass me. All of a sudden, everyone cleared out. I was the only one there. So I get in the car, turn on the radio. Well, a second one had developed directly behind me. And I could see it. I hadn't bothered to consider the possibility there was more than one. So I had to drive to Meeker, almost to Prague. It was chasing me down the highway. As it caught me, I pulled into the Prague airport, into a low area. Hail was falling horizontally because of the wind. It skipped off the hood of the car. Then it became so black you couldn't even see the end of the hood. That was from moisture, black chunks of cloud moving by. Then it slowly lightened."

What makes Foster unusual is that he paints tornadoes and

storms from photographs he takes. By day he's a geological draftsman for an oil company, by night—as his family sleeps—he can be found awake after midnight, dabbing paint on a canvas. With varying amounts of success, he tries to replicate the luminous splendor of three-dimensional clouds. In his best works, the clouds suggest explosive movement and shine with an inner glow. Admirers ask if he rigs artificial lights behind them. That realism isn't a virtue when painting tornadoes for the public, he learned after selling his first painting of one. In a 22-by-28-inch watercolor, a red pickup fled a tumbling tornado as scud clouds flew in to feed the monster. Comments from observers stung him.

"I don't want that in my house."

"It's like painting a bomb going off. Who wants to see that?"

"I'd rather have a nude hanging in my house."

That last remark is particularly severe in the conservative Bible Belt, so Foster decided to tone down the harsh look of the twister in future paintings. In one recent work it hangs in the far background from a rainfree base, but looks almost ornamental, with no sign of rotary motion. It could be brushed out with little adverse effect on the composition.

Since Foster generally limits his storm chasing to a one-county radius of his home, and even then waits until a tornado warning goes out, he would be considered by many a "gentleman chaser." At the other extreme are insatiable addicts who structure their lives around the seasonal outbursts of cruel Oklahoma weather. They have earned a reputation for being where the storms are, no matter what the personal cost.

Marty Feely, for example, hails from San Jose, California. He took up the hobby relatively late in life. At the age of 29, his marriage was crumbling and his bad back forced him to retire from his job as a bus driver. In 1984, while visiting relatives in Oklahoma, he talked his way into a car full of college-student chasers. That day they saw little of great interest. Late in the afternoon, tired of being dragged all over two states, Feely wondered aloud in an irritable voice why they didn't just give up and go home.

Before long it was Marty Feely who refused to go home. Storm chasing infused meaning and purpose into his meandering life. It gave him an identity. For 10 months each year he worked odd jobs in California. He delivered newspapers, rising seven days a week at 3 A.M. He guessed weights at an entertainment theme park, caparisoned in a red-pinstripe suit and straw hat as The Amazing Alfredo. Every April 30, without a second thought, he quit his jobs to pack his bags for Oklahoma, where he spent May and June racing after thunderstorms.

This was the real career he wanted, so he puzzled over how to make it pay. Selling his original storm videotapes at a Colorado weather conference flopped, so he considered a rather unusual idea. He would offer packaged vacations, with a twist. Lots of weather lovers dreamed of seeing a tornado up close, but had no idea where to go or what to do. Marty Feely would be their guide, operating under the name Whirlwind Tours. The spring of 1993, his first year of business, his rental car rolled into the airport at Amarillo, Texas, every Sunday to collect a new batch of tourists.

What they got for $750 a week was transportation and lodging and a four-page contract holding Feely blameless for damage to their equipment, personal injuries, or death. Nowhere did he guarantee ever finding a tornado. Sure enough, despite covering eight thousand miles from Texas to Nebraska, during that first spring Whirlwind Tours caught only two twisters. One unpleasantly long spell of good weather landed them at a mall where, with nothing better to do, they hunted for books with photos of tornadoes.

Operating the tours has freed Feely to chase storms at any time of the year, a rare luxury. Jim Leonard of Florida, too, has arranged his life to achieve such flexibility. Like Feely, he has held down the occasional odd job, mowing lawns and delivering pizzas. His earnings have allowed him to jet to Guam for typhoon season to satisfy his peculiar appetite. His fascination with high winds surely qualifies as a mania. Leonard, a slim, quiet, unsmiling man with an occasional dark chuckle, says his attraction goes back to his boyhood in southern Florida, when he connected to violent weather on a visceral level.

"I was always interested in storms. The higher the winds got, the more turned on I was. When I saw a wind storm, I went crazy. That's why I got into hurricanes so much. I experienced

Hurricane Donna in 1960 and that was an experience. We only got 80-, 90-mile-an-hour winds, but it was awesome. I was 10. From then on, I tracked every hurricane out there. When you're in a hurricane, it's something you'll never forget, especially the stronger ones. When you get a Category Four or Five, some people, it'll screw up their minds for the rest of their lives. People are going to have psychological problems. But if you're into the storm like a chaser, it's exhilarating."

"Chasing" hurricanes—powerful tropical cyclones with rain and wind spiraling in around a central eye—is a brutish kind of thrill, stripped of suspense and nuance. Forecasting matters little. The trick is to be parked in the lee of a sturdy building as the hurricane rages by. And Jim Leonard never missed the passage of one if he could help it. Recovering from back surgery in 1987, he paced anxiously in his Florida hospital room all weekend. Nearing the coast was Hurricane Floyd. On Monday morning he blurted to his doctor, "I've got to get out of here." The doctor released him with strict orders to rest his back. Soon a carload of hurricane chasers was charging toward the Florida Keys to greet Floyd, Jim Leonard lying flat across the rear seat.

He has pursued tornadoes since 1974. Leonard likes to get close. Really close. In 1982 in Texas he encountered a half-mile-wide whirl. His tape recorder was running: "Hey, there's one now (camera gear falls, clattering) . . . Oh, wow! . . . Jeez, look at that . . . Hey, there's another one . . . I can't believe it! This is Tornado City! Oh, my God . . . Hey, that's too close . . . Jesus Christ, let's get out of here!" His best-of videotape includes a scene of large hailstones shelling an outdoor pool and stripping branches off trees, in what resembles a mortar attack.

Gene Moore knows the danger of being caught in a hailstorm. Moore, a former TV meteorologist and a fixture on the Oklahoma storm-chasing scene in the 1970s, has been beaten by hailstones until he bled. He used to tote along a motorcycle helmet to protect his head from them. Moore has also had a few close shaves with tornadoes. One briefly swallowed his car once.

"It formed almost overhead. The funnel was at a 45-degree angle so the debris cloud went up behind us and the wind switched and got extremely strong. It was about one hundred yards wide, not a huge tornado. I tried to outrun it. Visibility went to zero. Just dirt, black, the condensation. The yellow lines on the road went away. I was going a little more than a hundred miles an hour. The guy with me screamed—and I barely heard him, the storm was so loud—'Hey, look at this!' It was a dirty two-by-four, about a foot and a half from the outside window, just hovering there. Then I emerged on the northeast side of the funnel."

The reason Moore now owns an elaborate set of clamp-on tripods (for taking photos from safely inside his car) isn't because of tornadoes or hail, but lightning. About 15 percent more people die each year from lightning than tornadoes. Furthermore, lightning deaths and injuries are known to be under reported. This killer strikes with all the grace of a sledgehammer. Like a giant defibrillator, it stops the heart. It wipes out short-term memory, ruptures eardrums, separates retinas, and burns ear canals. It might leave a rashlike mark in the crook of an elbow, where sweat evaporates and turns to burning steam. Other burns look like small circles produced with a cigarette lighter. Some markings are feathery raspberry patterns on the skin reminiscent of the imprint of a magnetic field.

Every year, 50 million bolts strike the United States. On a May day in 1981, one of them struck Gene Moore.

South of Oklahoma City, he and two television crew members were videotaping a greenish-white tornado bent like a crooked elephant trunk, tearing apart trees two miles north. Where they stood, it was peaceful, no lightning or thunder. A few scattered raindrops fell from the thunderstorm anvil, then a loud, continuous buzzing drowned out the cheeps of birds. When lightning is about to strike, it's advisable to crouch low to the ground.

Moore, holding the camera, had no time for that. His hair floated straight up as he felt a charge well up through his body. He tried to say, "Oh, God," but was cut off after "Oh." Lightning forked down to a utility pole, then leaped to a barbed wire fence, then to him in a brilliant flash. He was knocked 10 feet through the air. Flying backward, he discharged a side flash, a pencil-thick arc with a hundred trembling ripples. It jumped from his hand with a pistol crack and knocked down another crew member. A man in the act of monitoring support equipment for

Moore's camera received a shock down the connecting cable and collapsed, his legs buckling.

After a few moments they all rose, wobbly and groggy. A nearby storm chaser who had foolishly grabbed the barbed wire fence ran away, howling and shaking his stung hands. Moore rose quickly, trying to prove he was unhurt. He felt awful and slumped back down. His body was numb from head to toe, tingling like a limb that has fallen asleep. The hair on the back of his hand was burned off. Worse, his ability to think was strangely muddled. He would look at a common object, like a sock, and process the image without being able to fathom what it was or what purpose it served.

The next morning each crew member awoke with harsh flulike symptoms of fever, nausea, aching joints, and weakness. Every muscle in Moore's body felt as if it had been yanked. He lived with the tingling sensation all over his body for two days. In the mirror, he spied strands of his hair that had turned gray. Still, it could have been worse, he realized. "It was of course not the mother lode. If we had gotten hit by the main bolt, we would've been fried."

This dramatic episode made its way onto the pages of *Stormtrack*. No matter what their motivations, diverse amateur storm chasers could agree on one thing: *Stormtrack* was their official publication. Even after upgrading to a glossy cover, it maintained an unpretentious, homespun look. It continued to serve as a catchall for all sorts of tidbits, everything from technical tips on making slide duplicates and shooting in low light to a news item that thousands of late-summer tornadoes skip across the surface of Mars. Dave Hoadley did step down as editor in 1986. He selected as his replacement Tim Marshall, a civil engineer and meteorologist for a Dallas firm that specialized in damage consulting after hurricanes and tornadoes. Marshall flew out to disaster sites. Then, like a detective, he carefully investigated how buildings broke apart and why. He possessed a calm and confident demeanor that seemed ideally suited to tracking storms.

It wasn't always so. Like Bill Hauptman, he once had a tornado phobia, growing up in Illinois. He liked taking weather observations as a Cub Scout and was elated to get a barometer

for Christmas, but storms both enthralled and frightened him.
He naively believed in a bit of weather folklore, that lightning in
a circle signals a forming tornado. When, his face pressed
against a window on a stormy day, he saw a hot white bolt curl
in a neat ring over the house, he recoiled in horror. Nothing
terrible happened, but two years later an event marked him for
life. The sky darkened eerily, the wind kicked up, and his family
rushed down to the basement. The threat passed, then the sound
of sirens pierced the cool darkness. At school the next morning,
there were empty chairs. Some classmates had died in the tornado.

April 21, 1967.

"After that I had nightmares. If your town is hit by a tornado, and you have some friends that never show back up at
school, it makes a lasting impression. Any dark cloud that came
over the house, any cumulus cloud, I'd run next door to the neighbor's basement. It was a fear of the unknown. That's what
turned into the driving motivation I have: a fear of the unknown.
I learned how to turn that fear completely around."

He caught storm fever in graduate school, after relocating to
points south. For his studies, he attended Texas Tech University,
which happens to lie in the tornado-prone Texas Panhandle.
While there, he met a woman who understood his passion. At a
picnic with his future wife Kay, he persuaded her to chase a
nearby storm with him. They tracked down a rope tornado, a
fiery orange in the fading daylight. "Holy cow, look at that!" she
screamed. At that moment, Marshall says, he knew he was going
to marry her.

That was 1982, a memorable year also for the mightiest
supercell he has ever witnessed, a "mega-supercell." Its explo-
sively powerful shape resembled an atomic mushroom cloud. The
tightly wrapped updraft looked like a rotating barber pole. A
razor-edge, dense anvil completely blotted out sunlight. Fortunately for those in its path and for photographers like Marshall,
it was a sluggishly moving giant. Near Pampa, the same Texas
town that the Woodward tornado barely missed, eight twisters
then touched down, one after another, starting at six in the
evening. The spectacle lasted for two and a half hours. Marshall
took five hundred photos, shot an hour of movie footage, then
ran out of film as yet another tornado coiled down.

Such an experience comes once in a lifetime, even for the most committed storm chaser. It's usually the culmination of a long day. Early in the morning, Marshall plots out a jumble of data from balloon soundings and weather service offices all over the Southern Plains. His final maps look, to the uninitiated, like a kind of hieroglyphics. To him they contain messages and clues about how that day's weather will shape up. He notes the location of swirling low-pressure troughs and various jet streams, and factors in dew points, overcast and clear regions, strong surface winds, and maybe a dryline setting up or a cold front sliding through.

"There's a challenge to myself. It's a mental challenge: 'Can I forecast this?' There's nothing more satisfying than forecasting the storm, driving ten hours to witness its birth, the tornadoes that follow, then the demise of the storm. That's the ultimate success. The forecast is half of it."

The challenge of forecasting is often overlooked as one of the attractions of storm chasing. Also overlooked are the quiet moments that possess a simple beauty. Dave Hoadley enjoys describing how he burst through a column of rain to behold a field of barley, drops of water sparkling in their beards like thousands of tiny diamonds. This gentler side of the hobby helps soften the rambunctious, thrill-seeking stereotype. It still does not, however, quell the indignation of those who find this activity obscene.

After all, the same focused power that makes storms so remarkable also kills and destroys. Broadly viewed, their existence can be defended. Their rains fill depleted reservoirs and soak the ground with life-sustaining water. Even lightning belongs to the cycle of life by fixing nitrogen in the soil for plant growth and starting forest fires that clear out deadwood. But the tornado, the crown jewel for the storm enthusiast, wrecks without any sort of redemption. Do we need tornadoes for anything? Probably not. Realizing this, and unable to reconcile a love of storms with a dislike for their destructive ways, more than one guilt-wracked chaser has laid down his camera and simply walked away.

Then again, tornadoes will not be wished away, and nowhere is that understood in a pragmatic sense better than in Oklahoma. Facing the threat means being both prepared and, more importantly, forewarned. There is no hope of winning a showdown with an F5 tornado; the hope lies in not being dozing in the armchair when it savages your neighborhood. In this regard, professional and amateur storm chasers have made a difference. They donated hundreds of slides to seminars for training storm spotters. They managed to peel aside some of the veils shielding the secrets of the tornado. They relayed essential ground-truth information crucial in developing Doppler radar. They enabled storm modelers to incorporate doses of reality into their hypothetical, number-heavy computer simulations, to improve the models and prevent them from taking fallacious detours. They used their expertise at work, on the front lines of forecasting, to predict if a certain storm was going to produce tornadoes or simply lots of hail.

Another way of looking at it is this: People need all the observational nets they can get against a fast-striking terrorist. Statistically, on average a tornado occurs at a given spot in Oklahoma once every 1,980 years, which at first seems to be a risk of infinitesimally small proportions. Yet one day, for the smallest town in the most remote region of the state, the smothering, whipping ground cloud will move in. No one wants that to come as a complete surprise when it happens. People will take whatever warning they can get, whether it's from a Gary England with a high-tech radar, or a college-age storm chaser tooling a clunker down an old farm road, trying to get a good look at a lowering wall cloud. No one wants to be caught dry mouthed and helpless on the porch, watching as a tall black funnel rushes closer. And no one ever wants a repeat of the horror that visited Woodward on a damp, windy day in 1947.

Afterword

Here are a few parting thoughts, for what they're worth.

When I first began doing research for this book, one angle I wanted to explore was the presence of a tornado culture rooted in fear and vigilance. I didn't really find it, at least not to the degree that I foresaw.

True, signs of being in storm country are everywhere. In an Oklahoma Radio Shack display window, you might see not a computer video game, but a gray cotton funnel advertising the Weatheradio. A boy sacks your groceries in a bag with tornado safety tips running down the front. School children crouch in long hallways in safety drills. A siren on a sunny midsummer day wails for a minute or two at noon sharp. It's just a test—this time. And, on the lighter side, an entrepreneur has a business selling a "pet tornado" that rotates in a sealed glass of water.

Still, ask an ordinary Oklahoman if living here makes him anxious, and you're likely to be met with an indifferent shrug. Most people don't get too concerned about tornadoes.

What then began to intrigue me was the rather subtle matter of how some of the smartest weather consumers in the nation perceive these vicious storms on a variety of levels. Some of the interplay of myth and truth I looked at in Chapter Six.

One myth I wanted to sneak in here, because it relates to the appendix that follows, is that of the "all-powerful tornado." Even some structural engineers I spoke with denied that much could be done to fortify a house against a twister. This myth unfortunately leads to a dangerous fatalism.

Its origins probably lie at least in part in an old belief meteorologists held that houses explode because of a vacuum at the tornado's core. This is untrue. Only a partial vacuum exists, and it's far less important than the fact that a violent tornado (packing 200-, 250-mile-an-hour winds) simply demolishes a house so fast it appears to explode.

The kicker is that very few tornadoes are that violent. On the average, the wind speed reaches only 100 miles an hour. And this amount of pressure, as a structural engineer at the University of Oklahoma by the name of Harold Conner has demonstrated, a normal house can resist.

Conner supervised students in an engineering lab who experimented with a hand-operated pump to stress roof sections. It simulated wind forces. The results? An eight-inch-long lag bolt connecting the rafter and top plate of the wall (adding enough of them would cost only a few hundred dollars) holds fast in a wind up to 160 miles an hour. If ordinary nails are used instead, the roof section flies apart in a mere 70-mile-an-hour wind. Long lag bolts would protect a roof against 92 percent of all tornadoes. Securing the roof, a major unifying structural element, means perhaps saving the entire building.

Despite these remarkable findings, Conner has been frustrated. Homebuilders have shown little interest in his study and in making even simple structural improvements. Maybe some myths just die hard.

Some mysteries certainly do. Remember Joan Gay Croft, the blue-eyed, four-year-old blonde missing after the Woodward tornado? In the fall of 1993, NBC-TV's *Unsolved Mysteries* aired a segment about her case. Dozens of calls poured in from women who claimed to be the long-missing child. One woman, from Phoenix, Arizona, buoyed the hopes of Joan Gay's relatives.

She said that as a child she had flashbacks of strange faces and people. Much later, she underwent hypnosis therapy and memories streamed forth of dead and bloody bodies, of a hospital, of anguished moans and screams. The Associated Press even wrote an article about what seemed to be the resolution of this decades-old mystery.

It was not to be. A DNA test has virtually ruled out the Arizona woman as a relative of surviving Croft family members. And so a tornado, once again, leaves many questions in its wake. What really happened to Joan Gay? I don't know. Perhaps none of us ever will.

Appendix

Tornado Safety Tips

A **tornado watch** is the first level of alert to take notice of. It goes out in the form of a parallelogram-shaped box covering about 25,000 square miles (a little larger than one-third the total area of Oklahoma). A tornado is considered likely to touch down in this box within one to seven hours.

A **tornado warning** is the next, and highest, level of alert. It is made for a small area directly in the path of a tornado either sighted by spotters or indicated by radar.

(Note: For a number of reasons, radars can be unreliable in detecting tornadoes, especially from greater distances.)

General Safety

Think low. Wind speeds of the tornado increase with height.

Tornadoes usually cause blunt-force injuries from flying debris, so wrap yourself in a blanket or mattress. Take care to protect your head. One expert has even suggested investing in a motorcycle helmet.

In any kind of building **stay away from windows**, and from west and south walls. Almost 90 percent of Oklahoma tornadoes approach from the west, south, or southwest.

Remember that a tornado is most likely to be in the portion of the thunderstorm adjacent to large hail.

Where to Seek Shelter

At Home

Usually the **basement** affords the best protection (unless the ceiling is weak or the house is made of brick or stone, in which case there is the danger of being crushed if the building collapses). Good places to be in the basement:

An interior room
Under sturdy furniture like a heavy workbench
Under the stairway
In the middle of the basement floor

If you don't have a basement, take cover (under furniture, if possible) in a **small, central room on the lowest floor**. Look for a bathroom or closet.

In Offices or Schools

Go to an **interior hallway on the lowest floor**, or to a designated shelter area. Avoid auditoriums or gymnasiums. A wide, free-span roof can be whipped away by a tornado like a sheet of paper.

Do not take shelter in halls that open outdoors to the south or west.

In a Moving Vehicle

Do not try to outrun a tornado, especially if you are only guessing as to its speed and direction of movement. Stop, get out, and think low. Drop into a ditch, ravine, or gully, and lie flat. If you climb into a culvert, be aware of the possibility of flash floods.

Never stay in a mobile home. This kind of structure is extremely vulnerable to high winds. Either go to the park storm shelter or venture outside and look for low, protected ground.

(Note: Mobile homes have wrongly earned a reputation for being "tornado bait." Why? Probably because of the simple fact that, against a given intensity wind, a trailer park fares much worse than a comparable neighborhood of wood-frame houses. News reports further perpetuate the "tornado bait" myth by emphasizing dramatic examples of a tornado's impact—not a few unshingled roofs of sturdy homes, but rather a flattened trailer park or two.)

Glossary

Anvil: an ice-crystal apron of cloud that spreads downwind from the upper body of a thunderstorm.

Cumulonimbus: the huge, towering thunderstorm cloud.

Dew point: the temperature at which a certain parcel of air is moisture saturated and produces tiny water droplets.

Dryline: a narrow boundary between very moist and very dry air masses.

Dust devil: a small, generally harmless, whirling column of wind, caused by unequal solar heating of patches of ground.

Funnel: a rotating cone-shaped cloud that hangs from a cumulonimbus base. It often signals an imminent tornado.

Jet stream: a narrow river of intense winds, usually at an altitude somewhere between 25,000 and 45,000 feet, with speeds that can top two hundred miles an hour.

Inversion: an unusual atmospheric condition in which warmer air overlies colder air.

Mammatus: hanging pouches on the underside of a thunderstorm anvil, often harbingers of a severe storm. They play absolutely no role in tornado formation, despite having a shape that suggests funnel clouds.

Mesocyclone: a spinning column of air, up to 12 miles in diameter, at the heart of some thunderstorms. It has a low-pressure center and inwardly curling winds.

Multiple-vortex tornado: a powerful, wide tornado that contains several vortices that sometimes spin around a calm, central eye.

Severe thunderstorm: an official category for a strong thunderstorm. To be classified as such, it must have 58-mile-an-hour winds, ¾-inch hail, or funnel clouds or tornadoes.

Stratosphere: the atmospheric layer above the troposphere. It extends to about 30 miles above the earth.

Supercell: an intense, long-lived thunderstorm.

Tornado: a violently rotating column of air on the ground.

Troposphere: the lowest layer of the atmosphere. It extends to about eight miles above the earth over the United States.

Updraft: a flow of rising warm, moist air that sustains a thunderstorm.

Wall cloud: a lowering below a thunderstorm base, often wheel shaped and marked by broad rotation. A few minutes to an hour after a wall cloud appears, a tornado may lower from it.

Waterspout: a whirl like a tornado, but usually smaller and weaker, that tends to appear over shallow tropical water, such as that of the Florida Keys.

Wind shear: sudden changes in wind direction and speed over height.

Selected Bibliography

Archer, Jules. *Tornado!* Mankato, Minn.: Crestwood House, 1991.

Bluestein, Howard. "The University of Oklahoma Severe Storms Intercept Project—1979." *Bulletin of the American Meteorological Society,* June 1980.

————, et al. "Doppler Radar Wind Spectra of Supercell Tornadoes." *Monthly Weather Review,* August 1993.

Conner, Harold W., et al. "Roof Connections in Houses: Key to Wind Resistance." *Journal of Structural Engineering,* December 1987.

Cotton, William R. *Storms.* Fort Collins, Colo.: *ASTeR Press, 1990.

Cronley, Connie. "Beautiful But Deadly." *Monthly Oklahoma,* April 1977.

Debo, Angie. *Oklahoma, Foot-loose and Fancy-free.* Norman, Okla.: University of Oklahoma Press, 1949.

England, Gary. *Oklahoma Weather.* Oklahoma City: England and May, 1975.

————. *Those Terrible Twisters.* Oklahoma City, 1987.

Felknor, Peter S. *The Tri-State Tornado.* Ames, Iowa: Iowa State University Press, 1992.

Flora, Snowden D. *Tornadoes of the United States.* Norman, Okla.: University of Oklahoma Press, 1953.

Fujita, T. Theodore. *U.S. Tornadoes, Part One, 70-Year Statistics.* Chicago: Satellite and Mesometeorology Research Project of the University of Chicago, 1987.

Galway, Joseph G. "Early Severe Thunderstorm Forecasting and Research by the United States Weather Bureau." *Weather and Forecasting,* December 1992.

————. "J.P. Finley: The First Severe Storms Forecaster." Parts 1 and 2. *Bulletin of the American Meteorological Society,* November and December 1985.

Gannon, Robert. "Tornado! How Science Tracks Down the Dread Twister." *Popular Science,* September 1973.

Grazulis, Thomas P. *Significant Tornadoes, 1680–1991.* St. Johnsbury, Vt.: Environmental Films, 1993.

Harmetz, Aljean. *The Making of "The Wizard of Oz."* New York: Alfred A. Knopf, 1977.

Hauptman, William. "On the Dryline." *The Atlantic Monthly,* May 1984.

Hughes, Carol. "Tornado Town That Came Back." *Coronet,* March 1950.

Inglish, Howard, ed. *Tornado: Terror and Survival*. Andover, Kans.: The Counseling Center of Butler County, 1991.

James, Louise B. *Below Devil's Gap*. Perkins, Okla.: Evans Publications, 1984.

Jennings, Gary. *The Killer Storms*. Philadelphia: J.B. Lippincott Company, 1970.

Kessler, Edwin, ed. *Thunderstorms: A Social, Scientific, and Technological Documentary*. 2d ed. 3 vols. Norman, Okla.: University of Oklahoma Press, 1983–1988.

Lane, Frank W. *The Elements Rage*. Philadelphia: Chilton Books, 1965.

Ludlum, David. *Early American Tornadoes, 1586–1870*. Boston: American Meteorological Society, 1970.

———. *The Audubon Society Field Guide to North American Weather*. New York: Alfred A. Knopf, 1991.

Marshall, Tim. "A Passion for Prediction." *Weatherwise*, April/May 1993.

———. "Dryline Magic." *Weatherwise*, April/May 1992.

McDermott, Pat. "Flash—Tornado Warning!" *Saturday Evening Post*, July 28, 1951.

Miller, Peter. "Tornado!" *National Geographic*, June 1987.

Moller, Alan, et al. "Field Observations of the Union City Tornado in Oklahoma." *Weatherwise*, April 1974.

Morgan, Bruce J. *Proposal to the National Oceanic and Atmospheric Administration for Support of a Work Entitled Tornado Research Project*. University of Notre Dame, 1971.

1947 Woodward Tornado, produced by K-101 of Woodward, Okla., 90-minute radio program.

Oklahoma Publishing Company. "Destination Disaster." *Cuff Stuff*, May 1, 1947.

Ostby, Frederick P. "Operations of the National Severe Storms Forecast Center." *Weather and Forecasting*, December 1992.

Rasmussen, Erik N. *VORTEX-94 Operations Plan*. National Severe Storms Laboratory, March 22, 1994.

"Severe Local Storms for April 1947." *Monthly Weather Review*, April 1947.

Snow, John T. "The Tornado." *Scientific American*, April 1984.

Stormtrack. (numerous back issues)

Weems, John Edward. *The Tornado*. 2d ed. College Station, Tex.: Texas A&M University Press, 1991.

Index